# HEDGES, STICKS AND BASKETS

*Welsh Crafts Series:*

1. **THE FLANNEL MAKERS**
A Brief History of the Welsh Woollen Industry
J. Geraint Jenkins

2. **DRE-FACH FELINDRE AND THE WOOLLEN INDUSTRY**
J. Geraint Jenkins

3. **WELSH SLATE CRAFT**
Alun John Richards

4. **TRADITIONAL SPOONCARVING IN WALES**
Gwyndaf Breese

5. **THE CORACLE**
J. Geraint Jenkins

6. **TRADITIONAL CHEESEMAKING IN WALES**
Eurwen Richards

7. **THE THIRSTY DRAGON**
Brewing beer, distilling whisky
and cider and mead-making in Wales
Lyn Ebenezer

WELSH CRAFTS

# Hedges, Sticks and Baskets

**Meurig Owen**

Gwasg Carreg Gwalch

*Published by Llygad Gwalch in 2007.*


*ISBN: 1-84524-067-7*
*978-1-84524-067-7*

*Llygad Gwalch*
*Ysgubor Plas, Llwyndyrys, pwllheli, Gwynedd LL53 6NG*
*e-mail: gai@llygadgwalch.com website: www.llygadgwalch.com*
*Printed and published in Wales.*

*Acknowledgements:*

*Illustrations are by Meurig Owen, Coleg Gelli Aur and Gwasg Carreg Gwalch*

# Contents

# *The author*

Meurig Owen is a writer of a farming background, who for two and a half years wrote a weekly country column, as well as an arts feature for *Wales on Sunday*.

For a subsequent ten years he wrote a weekly country column, as well as a farming feature for the *Western Mail*. And for three years a monthly farm profile for the N.F.U. journal, *Farming Wales*.

Among his published books are *Ways with Hazel and Horn*, (with Bob Gruff Jones), 1996; *A Grand Tour of North Wales*, 2003; *Gordon Wilyman Memoirs of a Welsh Halfbred*, (with Gordon Wilyman), 2004; *Brenhines y Bryniau*, 2005:

He is on the approved list of Welsh Academy public speakers on literary subjects.

Meurig Owen lives in St Asaph with his wife, Menna.

## *Acknowledgements*

My thanks are due to several people for their help and advice. On stickmaking, members of the North Wales Stickmakers and Llysfasi Stickmakers were particularly helpful as were Dafydd Davies of Llanddewi Brefi, Andrew Jones of Llanbedr Pont Steffan, Emyr Howatson of Denbigh and Len Porter of Deiniolen.

Aeryn Owen Jones, Dinmael; Craig Evans, Llandyrnog and Bronwen Harding, Carno as well as Allan Portas of the National Hedge Laying Society gave valuable hedge laying advice.

Marvin Morgan, Ken Griffiths, Jane Johnson and David Jones Bangor on Dee; Beryl Smith, Llanidloes; and Sally Goymer, Cheltenham, Membership Secretary of the Basket Makers Association put me right with baskets and willows.

General advice was received from Twm Elias, Plas Tan y Bwlch and Gareth Beech of the Welsh Folk Museum St Ffagan. To the oh so many people who spared me their time most of whom are mentioned in this book, thanks a million. To Rev Ieuan Lloyd and John Dod who loaned me their books and revealed their thoughts, accept my gratitude.

Finally to my wife Menna, ever prepared to listen and advise at all hours of the day or night with editorial and grammatical advice my thanks and love.

# *Hedges*

## Hedges Have a Long History

*Good fences make good neighbours.*
*How the hedge evolved over 2000 years, establishing farm boundaries as a functional necessity.*
*The importance of the Norfolk Four Course Crop Rotation and the often controversial Enclosure Act in promoting the hedge culture.*
*Government grants and the Tir Gofal Scheme.*

How true the old Welsh country saying *Cymydog da yw clawdd terfyn,* A good boundary ditch makes a good neighbour.

The Welsh *clawdd,* is usually associated with the hedge, bank and ditch which marks out a farmers territorial right of ownership and responsibility. So it's a folk truism which is valued by all owners of land in the country.

Effectively a good *clawdd terfyn,* ensures that the farmer's livestock are in their rightful place: straying sheep are the bane of a shepherd's life and is one of the greatest causes of friction among country folk.

The planting of new hedgerows started in Britain during the Roman occupation about 2,000years ago and continued on and off through to the 18th century and the great spurt of the Enclosures Act .

All this developed, so to speak, from the ridge and furrow division of land which began in the 9th century. Often this would amount to a land length of 220 yards – a furlong – (a derivative of a furrow) and 22 yards wide. The furrow was the boundary. It is easy to see how such land allocation could work, as farmers tilled their land. Primitive ploughs drawn by horses or oxen could work the land, normally 30 acres per family. It is of interest here to consider that the horse collar, invented in China in the fifth century was first used here in the tenth century and replaced the harness band which had the drawback of pressing on the animal's windpipe. This was considered to be one of the most important inventions in the history of agriculture because it meant that horses could be more gainfully employed, being stronger and quicker than oxen.

*A freshly layed hedge*

In the annals of farming history we should note the bad weather of 1314, 15 and 16 with a slight recovery in 1317, and how this led to famine conditions for both man and beast, partly leading to the black death of 1347 which killed off one third of the European population.

History records renewed outbreaks of the pestilence for the remainder of the century resulting in a few scattered peasants grubbing a scanty living in the grimmest isolation, such were the effects of disease on the rural working population.

However, fast forward, to 1600 to 1800 and we see extremely important developments in farming which was eventually to stimulate hedgerow planting. This was what is known as the Norfolk Four Course system of crop rotation. Wheat was grown in the first year, followed by turnips in the second, then barley with clover and ryegrass under-sown, which was grazed or cut for feed in the fourth year. As land fertility improved, livestock and cereal crops also went up a gear.

Jethro Tull (1674-1741) the acclaimed inventor of the seed drill, was part of the new farming moves in his native Berkshire, sowing crops in rows and publishing *The Horse Hoeing Husbandry*, in 1733. Thus wheat was sown in rows and the horse drawn hoe destroyed the weeds. Other inventors followed.

The turnips fed to cattle during winter months in yards, and to sheep in folds, produced large amounts of manure. Sheep through their droppings and urine fertilized the land, resulting in heavier cereal crops.

This development put paid to the strip and open field system because livestock needed grazing space to glean the aftermath of harvest time.

Thus began the enclosure (not without a degree of enmity) as open land was corralled and hedges planted: some 6m acres from 1700 – 1845 (although it has to be said that by 1700 some two thirds of the land was already enclosed). This chimed in with a rapid population growth in England and Wales, from seven million in 1750 to over twenty million in 1850. Indeed the 18th and 19th centuries saw a revolution in crop yields, rotations and land improvement. This was an age of industrialization with a steady migration to the towns where people worked in cotton and woollen mills as well as quarries and mines. Yet the nation was fed without the benefit of large amounts of imported food.

It was a development which was to continue during the Napoleonic Wars, when besieged Britain was threatened with starvation, although many hedges were also uprooted and removed.

During the 20th century as farm mechanization gained a pace, fields were enlarged by hedge removal and gateways widened. During the 1960s the practice of stubble burning in some of the corn growing areas destroyed many hedges too, a practice made illegal in the 1980s.

In 1982 with the introduction of the Farm Capital Grants Scheme which offered subsidies for hedge planting and renovation, there was evidence of a positive government attitude.

There is no gainsaying the importance of good, well maintained

'There are few hedges [in Meirionnydd], dry-stone walls being the most common fence, some of which are built ar high as 6 feet, with broad coping stones, projecting 6 inches, which however do not prevent the sheep from getting over them. They are so active that they run up the walls like a squirrel, especially when their pasture turns bare.'

Culled from *General View of the Agriculture of North Wales* by George Kay (published 1794).

hedgerows in farm management. They control livestock grazing, confining animals to their allotted fields as well as providing them with wind breaks and shelter in stormy weather.

Government and their agencies in Britain have now fully realized the importance of hedge maintenance and management: on environmental grounds the ecological balance is sustained; as a beautifying feature of the countryside it has its attraction for the tourism industry, all this is in addition to the commercial advantages to the practicing farmer. Thus we find in various ways how government, in line with public opinion, is encouraging country people through financial grants and schemes to refine their expertise in hedge management. Later in this publication you will find sources of advice, schemes and grants which are actively promoted in Wales through the Countryside Council for Wales with their *Tir Gofal*.

This book will tell you precisely how the work is carried out and the tools that are required to do the job.

*In 1810 a General View of the Agriculture and Domestic Economy of North*

*A well layed hedge will control livestock and provide shelter*

*Wales, was drawn up and published by order of the Board of Agriculture and Internal Improvement, which urged in a reference to northern Wales, 'that the farmer should adopt, where it is practicable, the Norfolk rotation of turnips, barley, clover, wheat, & c, as part of a programme of hedge planting. The farmers would find their advantage in pursuing such a system of husbandry, exclusive of the benefit derived from the fences', it concluded. It is of interest to reflect that the memorandum was drawn up by Walter Davies, A.M. Rector of Manafon in Montgomeryshire from 1807 until 1837 and better known as Gwallter Mechain for his literary attainments. Such sentiments would no doubt be fully endorsed by R. S. Thomas, the world acclaimed poet, who was a much later incumbent of that parish from 1942 until 1954.*

*The Norfolk Four Course Crop rotation system is still well respected as a method of farm husbandry since it controls weeds, avoids plant diseases as well as providing a rest period for the land. Additionally peas, beans or clover in a rotation provide, through their root systems, nodules of nitrogen which can be taken up as a plant nutrient for a corn crop in the following year. In these times of mono culture and reliance on sprays for weed and disease control it is a system that is probably now ready for greater acceptance.*

*Some styles use pleated hazel lengths along the top as in this Brecon way shown here.*

# A Farmer is Judged by the State of His Hedge

*Good hedges a farm priority.*
*Hedgerow management.*
*Tools for hedge laying and a general job guide with a reference to regional styles.*
*Understanding the language!*

We have noted the development and importance of a good hedge. A farmer is often judged by the condition of his hedges. On taking up a new farm the state of the hedges will be of prime importance to the incomer. Before he can bring his livestock on to the land, first of all he will check out the condition of the outer fence. Straying livestock are the commonest cause of friction and agro in a rural community. In farm management it is important that the cattle are still in the meadow and not chomping in the corn – worse still if it's the neighbour's crop!

So a well hedged farm is the farmer's hallmark of excellence, his life is that much easier and he sleeps better in his bed at night. Hedges need to keep both cattle and sheep within the confines of their allotted fields. On the modern lowland dairy farm where the milkers graze from Spring until Autumn, then make way for tack sheep from the hills to graze off the roughage in Winter, good hedges are paramount. For a certainty those ewes, used to roaming on an open mountain will check out the hedge. That will be their priority! Be sure they'll find that one weak spot, and in two ticks there'll be one cheekier than the rest ready to push through and the rest will follow. It matters not that the lowland grass is that much sweeter than the mountain feg they've left behind, for one week they'll storm that hedge!

That's how good the hedge must be, ready to withstand the idiosyncrasies of livestock large or small in all weather. But also a good hedge will provide shelter against a cold driving wind, which is what a barbed wire and pig netting fence can never do. So caring for the hedge needs to come top of the work list.

The tractor mounted flail hedge trimmer does a quick and tidy job if done by a skilled operator. The cutting of the shoots stimulates growth and bushiness and should be done during the Autumn and Winter. This generally fits in well with the farm workload: harvesting is over – be it corn, root crop, or maize for the silage pit. Birds have left their nests. The flail will pulverize the trimmings and thus provide a mulch for the hedge plants as well as habitat for insect and mammal life. The one drawback being the possible adverse Winter weather working conditions when a heavy vehicle, such as a large tractor with a hedge trimmer attached, can rut and poach the land. But farmers are well used to overcoming that hazard. So the trimmer is the near ideal machine to preserve the hedge shape, maintaining a good width at the base.

But all is not freewheeling for the operator; trees growing in hedgerows fall foul of the system. While they may look well on a Constable or Turner landscape, for the hedge trimmer they are a bugbear. That part of the hedge adjoining a tree will have to be done with a sharp bill-hook or hand clipper. Indeed nowadays trees in hedgerows are best disposed of, because the roots of the tree going out into the field as they do, can spell trouble when the land is cultivated. Additionally the tree branching out creates a problem for the combine harvester, not only causing an accessibility problem but also an unevenness in the crop ripening for harvest. The same applies in grassland for haymaking and silage harvesting machines. The purists may argue the toss on this, but our concern here is for hedge management. Originally trees in hedgerows were a source of firewood to be periodically cropped by trimming of the branches. But now the ideal place for trees is in a plantation on land which is unsuitable for farming; an awkward corner of a field, an area where the depth of soil is shallow or the land is boggy. So if there is no restriction from planners or conservationists, this would be the ideal: remove the offending tree and plant hawthorn or blackthorn quicks in the resulting gap. And find the odd awkward corner on the farm to plant a pleasant spinney. These can be of more use to game and wildlife in any case than a few solitary hedgerow trees!

The flail hedge trimming regime can work wonders in stimulating, preserving and tidying the hedgerow. But there comes a time when a hedge section, as the result of the rigours of climate or molesting by livestock, becomes straggly and gappy. It is then time to consider hedge laying. Ideally the intended piece should be left to grow on for three years or more, before the work is undertaken. Some estates even rotate the hedge laying principle around the farm, thus dispensing with annual trimming, taking a different section in hand at periods of their choice. This has a lot to commend it because it's a system that offers good accommodation for wild birds. Pheasants find easy refuge. By slowing the

*A general clip with a sharp bill-hook completes the job*

wind it creates its own micro climate and raises the air temperature. These conditions can certainly fit well into particular farm schemes.

Basic hedge laying in principal is both easy and enjoyable. Anyone of average competence with hand tools can do it. It's a kind of work that can be done at whatever pace you like, pitting your wits in contemplative style against the elements of nature. Your challenge is often to transform a straggly overgrown waving wilderness into a stock proof barrier. Are you up for it?

Let's first of all consider the equipment that will be required. It goes without saying that the clothes you'll wear should be tough; hedging is particularly hard on what you wear, and that goes for footwear and headgear as well. Wellingtons are soon punctured, so strong leather boots are essential, and a hard wearing cap on your head for protection and warmth! A good boiler suit for ease of movement, thick tough leather hedging gloves and leather knee pads complete your protective clothing.

**Now for the tools that you need:**

**A bill-hook**. There are regional variations, but most hedgers now go for one with a ten inch blade. If there is a choice in your ironmongers, then

*Stakes ensure a firm and tidy hedge.*

it's worth trying them out for preference. Considerations should be given to the feel and length of the handle as well as its weight and balance in your hand, bearing in mind that this will be your most frequently used tool in hedge laying. It has to be comfortable in use and should not unduly tire your wrist, ideally therefore the handle should be fairly short and shaped nicely to fit into your hand.

**Axes.** Ideally your tool kit should include two axes, one being a light two to three pounder with a two foot six inch handle, and the other around five pounds with a longer handle; generally you'll find in the course of a day's hedging that both will come in handy.

**Trimming Hook or Sickle.** These generally have a two foot to two foot four inch blade, and are used mainly for brushing the hedge. Also useful is the long handled trimming hook or slasher.

**A Band Saw.** A small triangular twenty one inch band saw is handy for awkward corners, while the thirty inch one can be used for larger stuff as a cross-cut. Chain saws are sometimes used, but the utmost care in their use is advised because of the difficult conditions in which they are likely to be operated. Generally a band saw or axe will do a better job and be safer.

**A Small Sledge Hammer and Crowbar.** These will be needed for the stakes; the crowbar to make suitable holes in the ground, the sledge hammer to knock them in. Two inch by two wooden stakes should be on hand for positioning the hedge as work progresses and placed in bundles at eight yard intervals for convenience. These may be purchased from a timber yard, or alternatively strong hazel saplings may be found growing in a copse on the farm and cut accordingly. If the latter can be discovered having a natural hook then so much the better: they can be used to peg the hedge down securely.
**Carborundums**. A flat nine inch sharpening stone is advised to keep your blades in trim. And as an essential back up, make sure that you have a double electric drive grindstone, one being finer than the other to keep your tools razor sharp. That's going to make your hedge laying work a whole lot easier.

Hedge laying should be carried out between October and the end of March and the object of the exercise is to rejuvenate hedges that are overgrown and gappy, restoring them into neat stock-proof barriers. Ideally the stems (pleachers) will be at least eight foot high. The first task is to clear the weeds and ivy, the rubbish, away from the base of the hedge to be burnt (litter such as tin cans, old wire and zinc sheets should be collected and loaded up for safe disposal, left lying around at random they can be a serious danger to livestock). The pleachers can then be angled thirty to forty five degrees. This is done by cutting the pleacher part way through as near the ground as possible, thus weakening it sufficiently so that it bends over to the correct angle in the hedge. The principle to remember here is that the sap travels upwards: that is the reason why the angle of the lain pleacher is critical. It should always lay up hill on sloping ground. The sap traveling up the stem will continue the regrowth in the pleacher. The enabling cut which has been made at the pleacher base will be no more than is needed to weaken it sufficiently to ease it over, allowing it still to have the bark and some of the sap carrying innards to ensure its continued growth. Any resulting stub should be cut off with the axe or bill-hook to eliminate crevices which may trap rainwater, and therefore careful shaping should be done. Trapped rainwater tends to induce rotting so a smooth job should be done in this region. That will ensure healthy re-growth at the base. As the work proceeds the stakes should be knocked in to firm up the hedge.

Meanwhile advantage should be taken of the coppicing and pruning principle in regard to saplings growing within the hedge. Gaps will inevitably occur in spite of the hedge layer's best efforts. These can be successfully closed by planting quicks young saplings which can be purchased relatively cheaply from specialist nurserymen. For anyone with a cursory knowledge of planting, it's simply a matter of bedding the hawthorn or blackthorn transplants in leaf mould and top soil with adequate moisture. And that is basically it, there are inevitably regional variations in style and manner of securing the hedge against wind damage but the cardinal points are the same.

It's a good policy to gather and dispose, by burning, all the unwanted rubbish extracted from the hedge as soon as convenient. Otherwise if left lying around, the grass will grow through it and the thorns will harden, causing untold difficulty. This can be done using a fork and rake, gathering it into a pile on site and putting a match to it. Alternatively a tractor and buck-rake will make very short work of it too. If the fire is on grassland then the ash, rich in potash, should be raked up for the garden. Meanwhile it is worth scarifying the scorched earth and scattering grass seed to restore the pasture.

Finally you should protect your finished hedging masterpiece from marauding cattle and sheep by erecting a fence alongside. For keeping cattle at bay, two strands of barbed wire tightly drawn over fencing posts at two and a half yard centers is enough, while for sheep, pig or sheep netting will be required while the hedge is strengthening and bushing up. If it's a roadside hedge, then only the field side need be fenced, while if the fields are arable and not exposed to livestock, no fence will be required at all.

As with all crafts the best way of all to learn is to work alongside an experienced artisan, in this case a hedge layer of some standing. This is easily done because here is a kind of job which lends itself to a second mate. You will learn in a relatively short time in that way, about how best to use the various tools, about selection of the pleacher and the depth of cutting needed to lay it as well as the desired angle. By keen observation you will also learn about coppicing and the part it plays in the entire operation .

Give it a go, hedge laying is challenging, but both enjoyable and satisfying too. Your first effort going solo won't equal the standards of the old masters, but with experience you should achieve a quality to be proud of.

*The hedge laying described here is basically a beginner's guide, a taster so to speak. For competition purposes there will be certain conditions stipulated. References to regional styles: for the sake of simplicity and avoiding the risk of complicating issues have been kept so far to the over-riding principles. But a short reference to some of them may be in order. Valerie Greaves ,writer of a handbook* Hedge Laying Explained, *recommended by The National Hedge Laying Society, claims that there are scores of different styles. And even in Wales over forty! Officially we can say that there are probably four main ones in Wales, with as many as you care to name of permutations. To a great extent it probably comes down to personal preference and the amount of natural material available in each locality. For example we have a Stake and Pleach, style which is widely used in Wales. What this refers to is staking the hedge along its centre with lightweight posts at distances ranging from two to three feet. The angle of the stakes will vary, the Brecon style for example, will have them at 60-75 degrees or at right angles to the pleacher with double binding along the top. Which*

*The cut to enable the pleacher to be laid should be near ground level as shown here.*

*means that strong hazel saplings of eight to ten feet in length will be threaded tightly between the stakes to keep the pleachers from springing up. But each county will vary in style as between preferred pleacher and stake angles. And not all will use binders along the top. Some counties will use hazel crooks to peg the pleachers down, while others will rely simply on the stake angle.*

*Crop and Pleach, is yet another style which is a kind of variant, but this time using some pleachers as a live stake, (crop), alternating if desired with an ordinary stake. Some argue that since the crop, is rooted this makes for a more rigid hedge.*

*The height of the hedge is yet another variable depending on the size of the sheep, in other regions whether the hedge is intended mainly as an enclosure for bullocks.*

*Yet another consideration is whether the style allows for barding, the inclusion of deadwood pleachers in the hedge: some regions would have no compunction about this, interleaving with live pleachers, believing this offers cover, for the live pleacher as well as room for the pleacher to grow as the deadwood rots away. There are others who would raise their hands in horror at the mere thought of it!*

## Glossary

A **pleacher** is a live stem cut and laid to form a stock barrier.

**Coppicing** is the practice of periodically cutting down trees almost to ground level, thus allowing them to regenerate.

A **stake** is a light post, normally two inch by two about five foot long, which is driven into the hedge to keep the pleachers in place.

A **crop** is a stem which is cut off where it emerges from the laid hedge and left to act as a living stake.

**Brushing** refers to giving the hedge a light trim to stimulate bushing.

**Barding** refers to closing gaps using thorn boughs driven tightly into the hedge.

# Hedge Laying: An Expert's View

*Profile of a professional hedge layer.*
*Keeping tools razor sharp, and how and when to do the work.*
*After-care and the need for a fence to protect the hedge from marauding animals.*
*Farm grants and where to get them.*

Aeryn Owen Jones has a personal obsession, he finds bill-hooks and old style leather gloves irresistible. He laughs heartily at the very thought. In his time he must have bought scores of them .

He comes from country farming stock, and since the farm was sold has become arguably Wales leading (and busiest) hedge layer. He had done some in his youth, working along side his late father John Hugh Jones at Rhafod, Llangwm, before managing the farm took priority and hedging became a back number. Hedge laying was once more revived when an old experienced hedge layer, his neighbour Dafydd Williams, Pen Isa'r Mynydd, Dinmael, gave him serious lessons. Working alongside old Dafydd gave him confidence and the eventual comment: 'You're every bit as good as me now,' from his tutor. Aeryn has lived up to that early promise, and still remembers a lot of what Dafydd Williams told him: Keep your tools razor sharp, and the how and when, hedge laying should be done.

So when the farm was sold Aeryn had a ready made job; even that is a misnomer because every day's work is a pure joy. Transforming hedges, in some instances gappy and hardly touched for forty years, into sights of sheer beauty.

That moment with destiny was all of forty years ago: now his fame spans a huge expanse of North East Wales and Cheshire. Aeryn's hedges are his trade-mark: tidy, level topped, stock proof and vigorous; for the grazing sheep and cattle they're a windbreak. Little wonder he's so busy, such craftsmanship was bound to succeed.

He sharpens his billhooks and applies linseed oil to soften his dyrnwil (special leather gloves for hedge laying) ready for work at the beginning of October. For preference he likes to start with the old badly overgrown hedges because in October they will still have sap in them and therefore easier to manage. Often he will try to bend them over from the root, certainly two or three inches from ground level. If the old straggly hedges are left until around Christmas they, in the dormant period, will be dried out and can easily snap when laying.

Hedges should always be laid up hill, and as steeply as possible, says Aeryn. This allows the rainfall to run off and will, since the sap travels upwards, ensure vigourous growth. To do this, using the bill-hook or axe, he will make a cut as near ground level as possible to weaken the thorn the easier to bend it over. While so doing he will also clear up any dead vegetation and weeds within the body of the hedge. Essentially his aim will be to close up any gaps in the hedge as he proceeds. If the hedge, through every endeavour still leaves a gap, even for Aeryn this sometimes happens, he will close it up with a rail, a temporary measure pending the farmer later planting thorn quicks there in the spring.

Aeryn stresses that his objective is to produce a hedge of three foot six inches high with a level top, where rainwater will wash straight through down to the ground. With this in mind it is essential that the cut made to lay the hedge is clean and will not trap any water. This means that, with his bill-hook, any crevice will be smoothed over thus continuing an uninterrupted incline .

He aims to produce a hedge which is fairly loose, that is, not over packed. This will allow room for natural growth and development. And to secure a tidy structure, he will have suitable two by two inch posts hammered in at an angle every two to three feet. The laid hedge will be threaded and kept tidy in this way. If he finds a naturally growing stake in the hedge he will use it, cutting it at the correct level and incorporating it to stabilize the general structure. Occasionally with straggly overgrown hedges, coppicing can be a possibility combined with the more orthodox hedge laying. This will mean cutting the stems angled outwards, to allow for water runoff, at an inch or two above ground level. This will generate re-growth from the base thus ensuring a good chance of closing gaps in the lower reaches.

His ideal hedge for laying is one that's been planted and left to grow on for five or six years, rather than one that has evolved over a very much longer period. A hedge of this kind may be laid at any convenient time between the beginning of October and the end of March and will not present problems during dormancy. He will complete the work by giving the hedge a very light clipping, which will stimulate tillering in the Spring. Then again in late July a further light brushing.

Aeryn remembers an old countryside principle which is still a worthwhile point to bear in mind. That it is best to lay the hedge when the

*Aeryn Jones shows how stakes are used in hedge laying.*

fields are arable, this means that for a year or more it will be free of the threat of being molested by farm animals. However fencing alongside is still a matter that Aeryn insists on because sheep, cattle or horses can undo all the good hedge work in next to no time! He recommends sheep or pig netting with a single strand of barbed wire along the top. Practical considerations will come to bear on the positioning of the fence and its height; horses with their long necks have a good reach so the fence needs to be of a sufficient distance from the hedge to take this into account.

A question often asked concerning the tools used is about the use of a chain saw in certain circumstances. Evidently this is not a favourite with Aeryn although he accepts that it has its place. If a chain saw is used he says, make quite sure that the oil on the cutting chain is perfectly clean, else it can affect the growing vigour of the hedge. And turning to the hedge after-care, he advises light trimming when the tractor mounted flail hedge cutter is used, and for preference the work to be done in late August while there's still sap in the foliage.

## Key points

*Details of farm grants under the Tir Gofal Agri-Environment Scheme for Wales, towards hedge laying, may be obtained by contacting Countryside Council for Wales, Maes y Ffynnon, Penrhosgarnedd, Bangor, Gwynedd. LL57 2DW Telephone: 01248 355 782. They can also provide a handy leaflet on hedge laying and a booklist for further reading.*

*Hedge Laying is best carried out between October and the end of March.*

*The hedge should be laid against the slope with the stem (pleachers) lying at 45 degrees or better; since the sap travels upwards this will improve hedge vigour.*

*The hedge should be adequately fenced off to protect it from marauding farm animals!*

*The hedge will benefit from a gentle trim on completion and a further light brushing in late July to stimulate bushing.*

# Are you ready for a course?

*Details of hedge laying training courses and how they are conducted.*

*They are normally run by Agricultural Colleges over a two or three day period during November / December and supervised by suitably qualified practitioners.*

*Useful tips about bill-hooks and suitable gloves.*

***We have engaged first-rate men, paying I think, twenty-five shillings to thirty shillings a week to the instructor. We give the instruction free. We find a man who instructs, and is able to take up and lay a hedge himself, and make a bank, and who knows how to put a stake in, and we take a man who is thoroughly competent, and a man whom the pupils know can do the work well.***
From the minutes of evidence given to the *Royal Commission on Land in Wales and Monmouthshire* (Volume 5) 1896.

Most agricultural colleges in Wales organize Hedge Laying Courses of two to three days duration during early Winter. The usual format is, they will call on the services of a suitably qualified professional hedge layer to take a class on site. His or her role will be to give a course of instruction to a maximum of eight people, which will equip them at the end of it to do a reasonably competent job and with further experience achieve a high standard of ability. The people who join the course will be of a wide range of interests and ages. And their reasons for attending goes from simply satisfying their curiosity, to taking it up professionally. Some will already be fencing contractors anxious to add another string to their bow, some, farmers or country people, who want to improve their skills. As Craig Evans, a course instructor in Denbighshire says, 'they will be all eager to learn and his first task is to tone down their enthusiasm!'

Their day will start at nine and Craig's first duty is to go through the health and safety aspects of the work. 'This is extremely important,' he says 'because the tools used will be very sharp and the working conditions at times difficult, so care in handling the equipment is vital. Added to that, since the students will be working in pairs, they will also need to take account of others as well. The other essential on his check-list will be the first aid kit.'

Next he will explain in detail what we're doing with the hedge, what we want to keep and what needs to be taken out. So at the start it's a matter of brashing the side of the hedge away. Once they begin they're off, whacking and bashing stuff down. Each pair will be on an allocated eight yard section, and Craig then needs to show them how to lay the first pleach, the angle required and how it works. I need to say that even though the cut into the base of the pleach is fairly deep, it is still alive. And I will have to stress that it shouldn't be forced over; it's got to come on its own with just a little bit of tension.

The training is all done one stage at a time, the next step being the staking, which he demonstrates. 'I won't give them a massive amount to do because, on the first day particularly, they will be under very close supervision,' he says.

'I find that having them doing the task in pairs works quite well, because it's quite a physical job and they can help each other. That's my way of doing it, other instructors may do it differently, but the basics are the same.'

Personal preferences and experience are parts of Craig's guiding principles, which is why the students end the course with a very sound working knowledge of hedge laying in the Cheshire/northern Wales Style. He describes his ultimate target as producing a hedge staked with hedging stakes no more than two foot apart, angled at fifty degrees. It will not have hazel binding, relying on a fairly tight weave of the pleaches to maintain rigidity. The height he will go for is three foot six inches with a reasonably wide base. 'I don't see the point of laying a very thin hedge, cutting lots and lots out of it just for the sake of making it easier for yourself,' he argues. 'I will lay as much into it as I can, that way the hedge will provide a good wind break and therefore a better shelter as well benefit wild life.'

Most of the students at the end of a three day course will be able to lay a hedge and it will live. How tidy it will be is another thing but in the big picture, that doesn't matter. The aim is to get the pleaches all angled the same, with experience that'll come. They'll know the basics, they'll know what they're doing, and when they make mistakes they'll know why it happened.

The basics are easy to learn, he continues, but you have to have a genuine interest in it. It's hard work with blackthorn, hawthorn and brambles in it. If it's a very old hedge there'll be heavy stuff to pull out, all done manually. 'People shouldn't expect to make easy money at it when you're whacked with blackthorn, you've got to be interested! You need to want to do it for the right reasons.'

A big part of the advantage of joining a course is the benefits of the received wisdom of an experienced artisan. Thirtyfive years old Craig, a professional hedge layer all his adult life, has plenty of that. Students will soon learn of the care needed in maintaining and using equipment. If a chain saw is used, the need for a chain saw certificate and insurance. As far as bill-hooks are concerned, he advises looking out for them in farm dispersal sales: he claims that the old ones which were made years ago by the village blacksmith are better than those made today. Goggles should be worn as well as strong leather gloves. Pigskin gloves are commonly used; while they offer good protection from thorns, they are however being stiff rather ungainly in use. 'I tend to use welder's gauntlet gloves,' he says.

## Key Points

***The going rate for a three day hedge laying course is £140.***

***For that, students will learn how to lay a hedge and know how to handle tools safely. Thereafter it's practice makes perfect!***

***Learning from a professional hedge layer lets the student into secrets of the trade, like knowing what gloves to wear, and where to buy the best bill-hooks.***

***Courses are normally held in early November and are usually advertised in the Agriculture College brochure for your region.***

***The course will commence at nine o'clock and continue until four thirty each day consecutively.***

# The National Hedge Laying Society

The National Hedge Laying Society was established in the early 1970s, the founder members being three hedge layers Fred Whitefoot, Clive Matthew and Valerie Greaves. They realized that soon the valuable skills of hedgerow management acquired over hundreds of years would be lost forever. They recognized the signs; there had been a decline during the 1939-45 war years due to the lack of suitable labour and changes in agriculture that placed emphasis on food production.

By the 1960s hedges were declining at an alarming rate. Lack of maintenance meant that hedges became tall and gappy with nothing at the bottom, in essence simply a line of trees. Many hedges were grubbed out to make bigger fields that could be more efficiently managed by larger machinery.

So these three hedge layers conceived the idea of setting up a National Society to enable the skills to be documented, and passed on to others. Competitions were organized all over the country. A National Competition is now an annual event. This is in line with their declared purpose to: encourage and train people in the craft of hedge laying ,encourage landowners in the conservation and management of hedgerows and to encourage the development of hedgerow management skills by research, training and competitions.

The Society has over 300 members, some are professional contractors whilst others practice hedge laying as a hobby, helping out as volunteers at many national nature reserves and conservation sites.

Benefits of membership include: A Newsletter and free entry to the National Championship event. Access to a wealth of knowledge and experience, and to approved contractors, the ability to advertise on the Society web page which is www.hedgelaying.org.uk

Legislation was introduced in 1997 to help protect hedgerows. According to the government agency DEFRA the decline has been halted and between 1998 and 2004 over 4000km have been replanted and almost 7000km restored .

Maintenance of hedgerows is now part of good farming practice and the skills of the hedge layer are in great demand .

The Patron is HRH The Prince of Wales, and Secretary of the National Hedge Laying Society is Allan Portas, 88 Manor Road, Toddington, Bedfordshire. LU5 6AJ Telephone 01525 873795, while the

*Hedge laying family at the hedging match in Caersws*
*(left to right): Berwyn Harding, son; with mother and father, Bronwen, match secretary, and Gwynfor.*

Secretary of the Welsh Section is Herefordshire farmer, four miles over the border from the Wales, Jim Preece (telephone 01981 570 281).

# A Day at the Hedging Match

'Aye, it's a good test,' says Wil Jones as he looks across towards the twenty or so competitors pitting their wits and strength in the All Wales Hedging Match at Caersws in central Wales. Wil, a hedging champion who comes from Trawscoed near Aberystwyth, is a judge here and learnt his craft on the Trawscoed farm. 'There was an old fella there who taught me: he was a good hedger,' he says. 'In my time I'd reckon to lay sixty yards in a day even on a big hedge like this.' He's retired now, 'I have terrible aches in my knees,' he explains. But that doesn't prevent him with his co judge in the Montgomeryshire style, George Price from Sarn near Newtown a contract hedge layer with his brother Donald, from keeping a very close watch.

So what's the most important thing about these hedges? 'Well, you've got to make them thick haven't you to stop everything so that not even a rabbit can get through. A lot of these lads are making them very tight, and that's the right way to do it anyway, the tighter the better. That's the way I was taught.' And what about the size? 'Its got to be four foot high when they're finished and as wide as you like in the bottom, using whatever you've got in the hedge. With a thick one like this it can be up to two foot six, tapering a bit towards the top.'

The trial hedge is the best he's ever seen with plenty of tall stuff, but he agrees that there's a lot to take out of it especially when you start. 'That's the first thing you do, take everything clean out, particularly the dead stuff.'

But what do these pros think of the practice of sticking dead, pleaches back into the hedge? 'Most of them are doing it,' George admits, and shows a special stick he has to pull them up in case it's overdone. But they're both agreed that it's alright so long as you have a live one underneath and a live one above it, because then the dead one protects the live one and as the dead, one disintegrates the live one flourishes.

But what do these guys think of the use of chainsaws? Both where brought up on the traditional razor-sharp axe, bill-hook and hand saw. 'That was the custom years ago but now with a chain saw it's much easier and quicker,' says George, 'you can poke it into a hedge, it gets to places you'd have difficulty reaching with an axe. It's all chain saw now. You can use whatever tools you like. But you've got to have the proper trousers when using a chain saw. If a safety officer came round and saw you

*Live pleaches can make excellent stakes as shown here.*

without your proper boots and leggings, he'd stop you straight away.' Here the stewards see to that. It's a point on which Wil is in total agreement 'Oh heck yes, protection for your face and the legs as well'. The trousers they wear now have thermal woolen protection, if the chain saw was to catch it – the engine would stop immediately. Otherwise the chain saw would go through ordinary trousers like butter. 'A chain saw can be a very dangerous tool. You only have to catch a twig and you can lose control.'

'The specially made trousers cost up to £80 those are the ones you must wear, and with hedge laying there's a lot of wear and tear on your clothes.'

The competitors will have to finish their eight yard section by half past two, then the judges will need to tot up their score sheets. But Wil reckons they will have a fairly good idea of the placings well before that. While George and Wil get their heads together over the Momtgomeryshire style the other judges on the Radnor & Brecon: Andrew Evans from Llandrindod Wells and Trevor Protheroe from Brecon will scrutinize their sections.

The overall champion on the day will be adjudicated by Arthur

Lloyd, a retired farmer from New Mills near Welshpool. He was taught the craft by his father Edward Lloyd, a good all rounder of the old school, 'and I've been in it since 1945'. Today he bears the responsibility of awarding the top accolade. He's pleased with the work that's going on. 'It's a good test,' he muses, 'a little on the big side, still we've got to take what we can get. Yes, it'll be a good fence at the finish which will last for many years.'

What about the content of the hedge there doesn't seem to be much hawthorn in it? He begs to differ: 'there's quite a lot on the far side,' he remarks, 'but a lot of it has been cut away if I was doing it I would have left them in. There's a fair bit of hazel in it which isn't as good hedge material, but even though the hawthorn has been cut it'll be sprouting up from the ground again in a couple of years.'

'Nice to see a few youngsters taking part in general there aren't many going in for this job,' he says, 'well, there's not many young people going into farming anyway, is there. Still the under 21 year olds class has a good entry.'

Tom Evans from Beula near Builth Wells at sixty four and with fifty years hedge laying experience is a seven times All Wales championship winner. 'And I still enjoy it, it's hard work but every piece I do is a challenge.' His enthusiasm for the competition shows no sign of flagging. So does he have any tips for a beginer? 'The main thing is to get a good teacher to start you right. I was very lucky, when I was thirteen I had a champion hedger from the village, Freddie Evans, and he started me off. He was an expert, particularly on a light hedge. He didn't like a big hedge but put him on a light hedge and he was well away. Then another champion, Milwyn Harvey came and taught us in the Young Farmers. He had the record for winning seven hedging matches on the trot – seven cups in the fifties against the best men. To do that then against people like Percy Mills, John Jones, Stephen Davies and Bradburn Davies; if you could beat guys of that standard, then you were really the tops. He taught us a few tricks and I worked for people around farms who were excellent hedgers. They would come by when I was hedge laying and show me an extra technique or two.' This seems a common denominator with most of the competitors that is, learning on Young Farmers courses or coached by experienced employers. This was so with Gwynfor Edwards, a frequent match winner from Cwm Maethlon near Tywyn, who learnt his craft while working at Pant y Neuadd for John Evans. 'My twenty two years

*Pictured at the Welsh Hedging Match – competitors needed to take out a lot of rough.*

with John Evans was the best college I could get,' he admits.

Geoff Stephens from Bridgenorth is a stalwart in the Veteran (65 years and over) class, and has competed since 1955. Along the way he's won the English National a couple of times as well as the Welsh Veterans. 'I've been hedge laying since I was a lad; saw the old boys doing it and decided to give it a go myself,' he says. Now that he's an old boy himself he can certainly show the younger ones a thing or two. 'I take pleasure in doing it, it's a good job, its not a burden if you enjoy the work.'

The Welsh Hedge Laying Match, which is normally held on the same day and location as the Welsh National Ploughing and Hedging event, was in 2005 and 2006 held separately under the auspices of the Hafren Hedging Society, at Caersws in central Wales. This was because of the availability of suitable hedges in the Hafren Valley and an active local committee to carry out the arrangements.

In 2006 the event was held on land between the A489 road and the Aberystwyth to Shrewsbury railway line on land belonging to Rachel Davies and family at Red House, Caersws.

Availability of a suitable hedge and location is crucial; here they had both. There was no need for a satellite device to find it either, merely antennae finely tuned in to hear the distant roar of chain saws at full throttle and point your vehicle towards the sound of gun fire! As you cross a couple of fields towards the source of action, all becomes evident: Land Rovers, Vans, cars and a tiny village of Ifor Williams Livestock Trailers before the scene of battle. Massively overgrown hedges where men in combat suits are sawing and hacking. This is where it's all happening the roaring brum-br-rump-brrum of chain saws is deafening. This is akin to jungle warfare!

The trailers accommodate the feeding arrangements and the secretarial base, the domain of the Secretary/Organizer, Bronwen Harding.

The unflappable Bronwen, always a smile mothers everyone; she manages to be everywhere and doesn't miss a thing, everything goes with clockwork precision.

The Hafren Hedging Society which celebrates it's twenty first birthday this year 2006 is run by a local committee of sixteen enthusiasts who meet at the Buck Hotel, at Caersws. Cyril Gethin of Llanidloes is the chairman, while Bronwen's husband Gwynfor Harding is vice chairman. Somewhere out there he's hacking away for the Open Championship, and son Berwyn likewise. You can't have greater dedication than that!

The committee also organizes an annual charity concert on the last Saturday in January at Llanidloes, usually raising about £1,500.

But that's not the only hat she wears because apart from all this she's a busy farmer's wife back in Carno, and is County Organizing Secretary of Montgomryshire Young Farmers, a flourishing organization of 800 country youngsters in a network of eighteen clubs. Her next project: arranging a Young Farmer's Hedge Laying Course; she already has thirteen enrolled and her husband Gwynfor roped in as tutor. You can't possibly say better than that. At next year's Hafren Hedging Match she's looking for a bumper entry in the Under 21 Class!

The Secretary of Hafren Hedging Society is Bronwen Harding, Delfryn, Carno, Powys. Telephone: 01686 420 606

***For further study read:***

*Hedgelaying Explained* by Valerie Greaves (available from The National Hedge Laying Society, 88 Manor Road, Toddington, Beds LU5 6AJ. Tel 01525 873 795).

*Hedging a practical handbook* published by the British Trust for

*Striving for a perfect finish at the Welsh Hedge Laying Match*

Conservation Volunteers. ISBN 0 946752 02 8

*New Hedges for the Countryside* by Murray Maclean. Published by Farming Press. ISBN 0 85236 242 0

*Hedge Laying And Fencing* by Edward Hart. Published by Thorsons Publishers Limited. ISBN 0-7225-0701-1

*Hedgerow management and renovation, a guide for land managers* An information leaflet published by the Countryside Council For Wales. ISBN 1 86169 020 7

*Hedges and Walls* by Tom Williamson. Published by The National Trust. ISBN 0 7078 0322 5

A 75 minute video *Laying it on the Line* which is a guide to the craft and styles of hedge laying is also available from the Society.

Courses are organized in hedge laying by agricultural colleges in Wales, and usually commence in early November

# *Sticks and Shepherd's Crooks*

## Refining an Ancient Skill

*An ancient skill celebrated by the bards is still*
*enjoyed and promoted by rural craftmen.*
*Tips on how course leader Emyr Howatson works.*
*What he looks for and where he finds it!*
*Horns of rams, buffalo and deer antlers can be used.*

Stick and shepherd's crooks makers have been around a very long time, part of a custom which goes back into the shrouds of ancient history. In Wales for example there is a playful reference to Bleddyn Ddu o Iâl sending a bardic missile in the 14th century to Comyn Coch o Fôn in a couplet:

*Yn gochel ddydd Marchnad*
*Gên ffon bugail mewn eiliad*

A bardic description of Comyn Coch as a frightened lamb quickly trying to elude the jaws of the shepherds crook on market day!

Sticks and shepherds, crooks still have their place, as much in poetic memory as in everyday use by country folk. Stickmakers are continuously refining their skill using methods very little known to their forebears and thoroughly enjoying new challenges.

* * *

Emyr Howatson's car is parked in the road outside his bungalow, Y Bwthyn, in Erw Salisbury on the outskirts of Denbigh. Where else, for goodness sake? His garage is jam packed with the paraphernalia of an expert stickmaker!

For ten years he was seconded by Llandrillo College to do evening classes at Ysgol Glan Clwyd in St Asaph. So there isn't much he doesn't know about the craft. The garage is an Alladin's Cave to delight any aspiring stickmaker. Bags of various animal horns lie around: rams, cows, buffalo and deer antlers, eventually to form the handles or crooks for the assorted sticks which are seasoning and maturing. And what an

*A stickmaking class at Coleg Sir Gâr, Gelli Aur, Llandeilo*

assortment: blackthorn, holly, ash, cherry, and his favourite of all, hazel because they are usually straighter. He has a favoured woodland where he can find suitable shanks, at Singrig near Llansannan the place where he once farmed, now run by his son since Emyr's retirement.

Even the less promising sticks can be straightened, he says selecting an unlikely holly candidate and reaching out for the electric paint stripper to show how a blast of hot air judicially applied, plus some gentle muscular pressure can work wonders on the shaping process. Another option is to apply steam from the spout of a boiling kettle.

The garage has even more at which to wonder: tools to fashion the horns and sticks, iron templates, vices, rasps of various shapes and bite, small chisels of sundry shapes to do the artwork and G-clamps. Also specially shaped blocks, not to mention simple devices Emyr has created himself out of old plumbers pipes, steel plates and touches of weld.

Another essential in his armoury is a deep pan in which to boil the horns sometimes for up to three hours, as is necessary with the particularly tough buffalo for example in order that they can be moulded into the shape he wants.

*One-piece hazel sticks – 'Ffon Sir Aberteifi' displayed by Andrew Jones.*

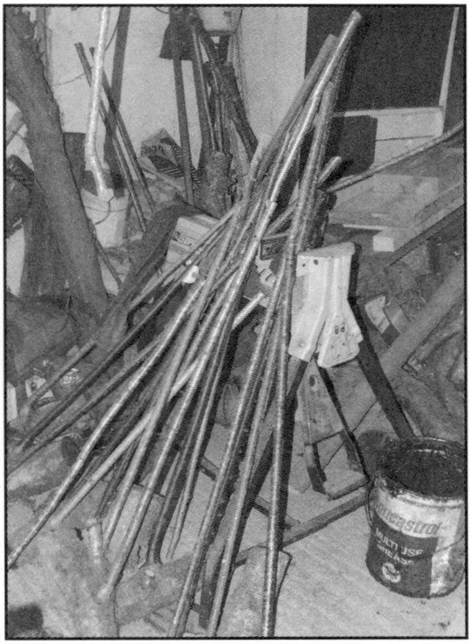

*A store of hazel sticks is essential in any workshop*

**Finding a Shaft**

The work begins by first finding suitable sticks, usually in mature woodland. Fortunately with his close rural Denbighshire links and Llansannan in particular, Emyr has no problems on that score. But as stickmaker Andrew Jones from Llanbedr Pont Steffan in Ceredigion advises, it is best to seek permission from the landowner before making your woodland search.

The astute countryman will often find what he wants while out walking. Coppiced trees such as ash, sycamore and willow which have been cut back low to generate re-growth often offer ideal material. Hazel too, especially strong saplings, are a delight to work on. But as Emyr points out, it is best not to cut sticks out of a hedge because they may be needed at some stage for when the hedge is laid. However, when hedge laying, often good material can be discovered amongst the discarded trash, be it black thorn, holly, willow or even hawthorn. And it is often worth keeping an eye open for material which includes a ready shaped root for the stick handle. While another possibility is a shank growing out of a thicker trunk which can be shaped with a band saw and sharp knife. So then, during the winter months before the sap has arisen and there's

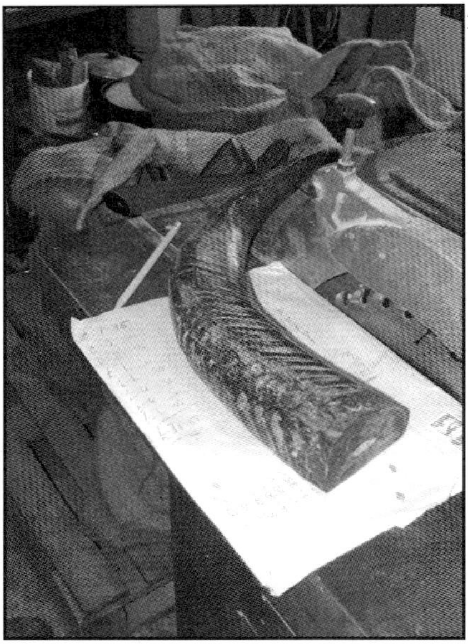

no

*A buffalo horn*

*A collection of Welsh ram horns*

foliage, the search is on for the ideal shank of a three foot six to five foot length: if there is a naturally shaped stick handle already growing, then this is a bonus. Always select shafts that are a lot thicker than you need, to allow for shrinkage during their year long maturing period. During November to January bare of any foliage they'll be easier to find and if they're discovered growing in stony ground, that will make for an even better quality stick and there will be good bark interest. Emyr uses a handy Stanley folding pocket saw, such as is often used by gardeners for pruning, to cut his selected sample. The other essentials are:

- A good sharp pocket knife, preferably one with a locking device for safety.
- A pair of secateurs or bill-hook for trimming off thorns and side shoots.
- A pair of leather gardening gloves and goggles, essential for handling holly or blackthorn.
- A strong trowel for exposing roots prior to cutting them.
- And finally lengths of baler twine the farmer's friend, to tie up your sticks in a bundle for ease of carrying. But bear in mind that freshly cut

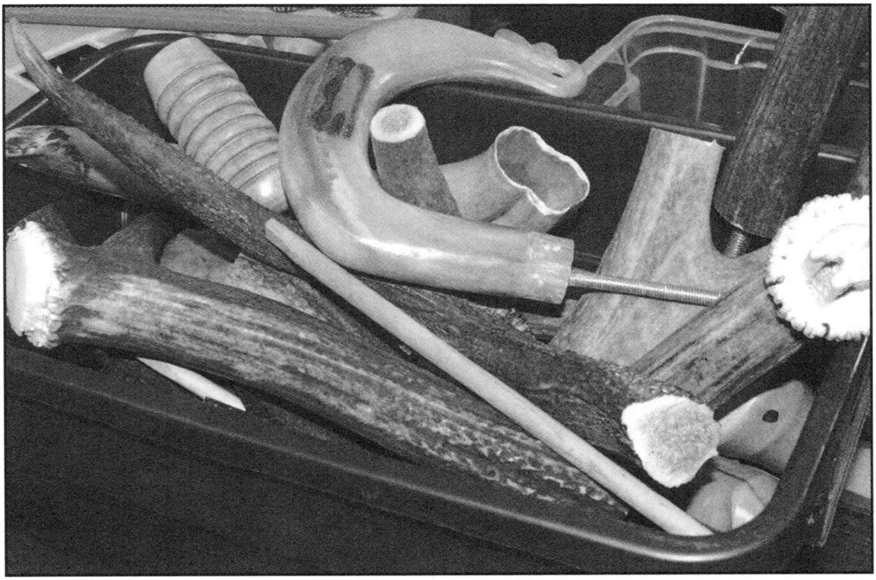

*A variety of horns and antlers*

sticks, even in winter, can be quite a heavy weight.

The sticks are then tidied up, cut into desired lengths and taken to the garage for a minimum twelve months drying and maturing period. Emyr offers the tip of standing them in a bucket, especially the hazel shanks: 'this keeps them free from woodworm,' he says. And another point worth making is to keep your cutting tools sharp: chisels, knives, bill-hooks and plains will then be a joy to work with. So practice your sharpening skill caring for your tools is always a good maxim.

**Horns for handles.**

'The horns are not so easy to come by,' says Emyr. The general practice of de-horning (dis-budding) calves at a few days old means that cattle horns have become very scarce indeed. Where once they were easily available at abattoirs, this is certainly no longer so. And since more and more people are taking up the stickmaking craft, the demand for them is increasing. While rams horns were once two a penny, from an upland farmer, they too canny folk as they are are getting a fiver and more for a good sample. Ewe horns such as those of the Scotch Blackface or Swaledale too make nice handles for the lighter market stick. Deer antlers, sometimes found in woodland, are a god-send to the stickmaker because they offer numerous possibilities, from a thumb-stick handle to conventional and more ornate ones, perhaps three or even more from the one sample.

The first thing Emyr does in horn preparation is to cut it across the base with a hacksaw so that it is free of any hollowness he likes to start with the horn intact, the inner core still tightly in place. He then boils the horn, typically half an hour for a ram's horn, then places it in a vice to bend it into the shape that he wants. The boiling will make it, given the application of modest pressure, more easily malleable. Also the inner core will come away, the more that comes out, the better. The object then will be to straighten the horn sufficiently to take a metal dowel or the prepared top end of the shaft as a two inch insert. That will depend on the size of the hole that emerges: if the hole is big enough and the horn is thick and strong, then the shaft end will be pared to fit in snugly with a generous application of cow gum or super glue to ensure a firm bonding. Conversely if the hole is small Emyr will use a quarter inch dowel to screw into the horn and also down into the shank, again using strong glue for a tight bonding (approximately three inches each way). In both instances it is essential that the fit is precise and firm.

Buffalo horn offers an exciting challenge: it is much harder to work on but the black mass opens up all sorts of interesting ideas in sculpted artwork; boiling time is three hours! But the general principles are the same for the stickmaker. During the boiling and shaping preparation you will be using various things to achieve your objective: the template to get the desired curve, the hot air gun always used on the inside of the bend, and as with Emyr, self devised tools to gently lever the horn into the way you want it to go. It is essential to remember not to release the horn from the vice or clamp before it has cooled down, otherwise it is likely to revert to its original shape

These are the broad principles of stickmaking. In the following chapters we will go into the finer detail, the nitty-gritty of this fascinating craft. There will be good days, and there will be the other ones when nothing goes right, it's that sort of science even for the expert, but hang on there for the masterpiece and the splendid sense of achievement. Let the next pages be your guide, they are the distilled wisdom of masters of the art.

# Getting Started

*Getting going on an easy option.*
*Progressing to a shepherd's crook and thumb-sticks.*
*Treating, shaping and fixing a horn handle.*

Your shafts have gone through the maturing period of at least a year in an airy part of your garage or shed, so we're ready to go! And since we're beginners lets start with a hazel stick – there's no point in looking for complications at this stage. The next matter to consider is what kind of stick you are going to make : there are various options – an ordinary walking stick, a lighter one for the market or a shepherds crook.

A simple walking stick will need to be about thirty-six inches long. If you managed to find a shaft with a nice nobly root formation attached to it, then you have a stick, after trimming off the side shoots, that is almost readymade. All you then need to do is to shape the root with a sharp knife or possibly cut back to size with a saw to form a knob or handle, and filing into shape with a Stanley rasp. Care should be taken lest you shave off too much, so easy does it. The final flourish will be to remove the score marks left by the rasp. This may be done with sandpapers, rubbing down using a course one to start with, then finer to bring about a smooth finish. The next thing to do is to cut the stick to size, here the length may vary according to the user but you should be safe cutting it at thirty-six inches (if its too long for comfort, it's a fairly simple matter to shave a little more off). Next fit on the ferule, these can be easily purchased in various sizes on stands at the larger sheepdog trials or they can be made by sawing an inch off the end of a half inch diameter copper pipe. Then you'll need to shape the end of the stick to accommodate it. This is done by making a shallow cut around the stick about one inch from the end using a very fine toothed hacksaw and doing the final shaping with a sharp knife. Having tried it out for fit you then squeeze the ferule on to the end of the stick with a couple of dents knocked around its edge for a grip. Or alternatively you can consider a neat rubber one to fit over the end of the stick. This is smart in appearance and gives an extra feeling of firmness when you're out walking. The straightening of the shaft can be done by applying heat with an electric paint stripper and then easing the stick manually into form. If the bark is attractive, then care should be taken to preserve it so that it will enhance the stick's final appearance. When you are satisfied that the shaft is clean, smooth and straight, it is ready for an application of yacht varnish and once that has dried your job is done. Ready for a country walk in great style!

Let us now consider various kinds of simple walking sticks. The familiar one with a rounded handle is another on which you can try your hand. The plan already outlined for our first stick will apply here too, but this time we will require a straight specimen (without any root attached). Here we will need a special template and the electric paint stripper to blow hot air where the stick handle needs to curve. Andrew Jones alternatively advises putting the part to be curved in steam for up to an hour and then, using the template both as a handle former and a source of leverage, gently try bending. Here care is needed because too much pressure can easily crack the stick. So it is a matter of fine judgment, recognizing how the stick is responding to the treatment and knowing when and if more heat needs to be applied. When the handle has come into shape, a cord is tied to keep it that way. The stick and 'bending roll' can then be taken away and left to cool off over night. The next day the cord can be cut and the stick gently eased off the 'roll'. This may cause some spring-back, but it won't be anything that the hot air blower applied in the right place can't rectify. And there you have your conventional walking stick.

You will see from all this, that with a little adaptation, we are only a short remove from creating a shepherd's crook out of a straight stick. For that ,of course, you will need a longer shaft ; nowadays trialists require that extra length for the final penning and the handle to be capable of accommodating a sheep's neck for catching. So bear in mind the way that the shepherd's crook will be used: create a crook that is big enough, will channel the ewe's neck into the cleft, yet will not injure the animal. This can be achieved using a longer shaft and allowing extra length at the crook. Then it's a matter of using the hot air method to shape the stick.

Another popular stick to consider is a thumb-stick, ideal around the farm or in the market for driving livestock, country walking or for using as a crutch to lean on. The same broad principles apply here too regarding the generalities of construction and finish. But for this we need a longish shaft topped with a naturally growing V. As the name implies, the user will hold the stick with his thumb comfortably in the V, so it's essential for the base of the V to be wide enough for this purpose. A V with a tight base can be shaved out and sandpapered accordingly, or using the hot air of the paint stripper, gently widened, but in doing so, don't over do it in case you split and spoil the shaft. Conversely adopting the same principle, by using heat, you can narrow the V by then putting it in a vice and closing it carefully with the pressure of the vice jaws. The length of the thumb-stick will be in the 50 to 55 inch range, (the length of the V spurs being 2.5 inches), much of this depending on the height of the user and his preferences.

**Sticks with Horn Handles**

Let us now consider sticks with horn handles, generally shepherd's crooks and the lightweight market sticks. Years ago Bob Griff Jones the great shepherd, sheepdog trialist and acknowledged stickmaker par excellence declared : 'Any old horn won't do for the handle. For a start try to get a horn off a ram that's at least four years old, that means that it will be long enough ; but with some it's possible that the nerve ends will have grown well into the horn. And again, for goodness sake try to avoid horns that have been heated and straightened when the rams were young. These will be hollow at the tips and have a blood clot in the horn'. So where did Bob Griff get suitable horns? If they weren't an endangered specie he would plump for horns of Jacob sheep ,'they make beautiful crooks' he said, 'but they no longer roam the land'. 'Here in Wales, luck is on our side', he continued, 'because the horn of the Welsh Mountain ram is the best we can get.' But even for Bob it wasn't all plain sailing. 'Horns are deceptive at best, and you can't be certain of their value until you have started working on them,' he concluded.

'I've worked for hours before now rasping and cursing – sweating pots – only to find that the horn is hollow, or there's a nasty dark blemish in the pigment. Some people are under the impression that you can make a handle out of any old horn – but you can't'. For Bob Griff 'a good quality horn of a Welsh Mountain ram, if you can get it, is unbeatable'. So there you have it, good quality horns are not easy to come by and the points Bob Griff made are very relevant as we begin our second stage of stickmaking. For the novice in farming practice, much of what has been described may sound strange, even far fetched. The old practice of training horns of show animals, in preparation for a good sale ring appearance, by heating them with a blow lamp is legendry, but can cause later havoc for the stickmaker.

So it's a matter of, first finding a good quality ram's horn and then locating the nerve ends. You will do this by carefully putting the horn in the vice and sawing across its base : essentially what you are doing is looking for the nerve ends, so it's best to take more than one cut – little by little, using your best hacksaw, until you find it.

You then need to boil the horn for about half an hour; in the interest of domestic harmony this isn't a job to be done in a saucepan on the Aga ! There must be a time and a place for all things, and the kitchen range is not one of them – the distinctive odour would permeate the entire house and your popularity rating would plummet to zero at a stroke ! So this is one for your garden shed or garage, full stop ! The boiling will release the inner core which can be easily extracted.

Next place the horn in the vice between two metal plates measuring nine inches by nine. The horn will be quite hot, so handle with care. Andrew Jones offers the useful tip of using barbeque tongs to lift the horn out of the saucepan, before letting the water drain off. The horn will still be hot so proceed with caution as you handle it. The horn will be reasonably malleable and the object of placing it in the vice is to get the curl out of it. When the horn has cooled properly, an important point this – because if it's removed too soon it will revert to its original shape curl and all, you can release it from the clamp. So you need to be patient.

But there's a lot more to be done to get it to resemble a crook handle. That will involve a vice, clamps, G-cramps, templates, formers and any other device that you have, plus focusing the hot air gun at selected parts of the horn to bend and coerce. Here, a word of caution – not to overdo the hot air gun in case it burns and discolours the horn. And not on any account to re-boil the horn – that would undo all the good work, causing the horn to return to its original form.

So how is all this done? Andrew Jones for example places the horn between the top and bottom formers and uses the vice to apply sufficient pressure to keep it in place. He then plays the hot air gun carefully along and around the crown of the handle and after three or four minutes tries tightening the vice a little. The horn then should give and begins to assume the shape of the formers. He continues heating and tightening until it does, but does not force it. 'If the temperature is right it will give way readily without excessive pressure being required', he says. As the formers close up on the horn, he will place the seven inch G-cramp and tighten up that too thus applying all round pressure.

Bob Griff too sometimes used a similar method with varying sized formers, at other times using a cord, a nail – windlass fashion – and a template, or on occasion a combination of both!.

To get the horn ready for the next stage, which is joining it to the shaft, there are a few more things still to be done. We need to be sure that the base of the horn, which will be the neck of the crook is long enough to take a two and a half inch dowel to make a firm join. This again can be done by making judicious use of the hot air gun, the vice and metal formers created by sawing a one to one and a half inch iron pipe down the middle. These can then be placed as a collar around the horn and put in the vice, and while plying hot air on the horn, gently closing the jaws. The effect of this will be to equate the horn to the diameter of the stick by closing down the horn and at the same time give adequate neck length for a metal or wooden dowel. Next day on opening the vice, you will see that the hole in the horn will need cleaning out. The objective now is to bore a 9/16th hole to accommodate a three inch dowel which we will create at the top of the stick. Care should be taken to do this in direct line with the shaft so that when we eventually bring them together the entire effect is seamless. It's probably best to begin with a smaller bit, say a quarter inch – if that isn't truly in line then you have at least a second chance to get it right.

Now lets look at the shaft because our next task is to prepare it to fit into the horn. So you have a suitably matured shaft ready, one of your longer ones. Our aim now is to match the stick to the horn, so for that we will create a three inch dowel at the top of the shaft in such a fashion that when they all come together everything will fit snugly, and the circumference of the horn and stick will be identical. So care and precision are the order of the day. Now to the practicalities : with a fine toothed saw or hacksaw, first cut off the top end of the stick nice and clean. Then three inches from the end, again with great precision, cut around the stick with the hacksaw; the depth of the cut being equal to the thickness of the wall of the horn. Next with a sharp knife, fine rasp and sandpaper shape the stick to fit into the horn. This achieved successfully, smear the insert with super glue or cow gum and bring together tightly. However way you can, to ensure a first rate bonding, make sure that the stick and horn are kept rigidly together until the glue has effectively gelled. There are further options as to how to secure a stronger bonding ,every person to his fancy. A quarter inch iron dowel joining the handle to the stick, is sometimes used. Or a four inch nail with the top sawn off may be used as an insert within the wooden dowel and down into the shaft. Bob Griff's personal preference however was the plain wooden dowel!

The remaining work to complete your shepherd's crook is now to cut it to length, as always, with a fine toothed hacksaw, the size being to the preference of its intended owner. We have already noted the requirements of the sheepdog trialist – a long stick for the final penning. That too is often called for by bishops in religious ceremonials.

The final flourish is the usual smoothing of the shaft, varnishing and fitting a suitable ferule.

# Stickmaking is a Way of Life

*Stickmakers lead a fulfilled life – and are very clubbable!*
*Len Porter, leader and pro at the North Wales Stickmakers Club, is inspirational.*
*More tips and wrinkles about shaping the horn, and how Len sculpts a leaping salmon.*

When someone once said to former Liverpool Football Club manager Bill Shankly that soccer was a matter of life and death, he said: 'Listen, its much more important than that!'

The same might well be said for the practitioners of stickmaking: to enter that community is to experience the frenzied excitement of the challenges it presents. Typically Len Porter, a professional fitter with the Gwynedd Health Authority in northern Wales, is a good example of the breed. When he's home at Penisa'r-waen the relatively isolated village at the foot of Snowdon, his work keeping the technical wheels of the regions N.H.S. sweetly turning finished for the day (but still on emergency standby), you can be sure that he's eating, drinking, talking and dreaming

*Len uses a clamp to bend the horn.*

of sticks. That is, when he's not in the *cyt*, at his work bench. *Cyt* is his playful word, normally used in the Welsh countryside for a small calf rearing outhouse, to describe the tiny workshop. Len has two!

Hardly surprising then that he's at the hub of the North Wales Stickmakers Club/Cymdeithas Gwneuthurwyr Ffyn Gogledd Cymru who meet monthly for an all day session at Glynllifon, the Meirion Dwyfor College near Caernarfon. Here they have the college facilities, work benches, power points and vices at their disposal.

The club membership, numbering over a hundred with an age range from eleven years old to over seventy, come from all the northern counties of Wales. The secretary and editor of their quarterly journal, *Y Fagl*, – which loosely translates as shepherd's crook, is Ray Jones from Penmaenmawr. While Len Porter, the club mentor in chief, is the cheer leader proffering valuable advice. He's the star performer, all action, all talking and with his massive box of tools, ever ready to lend a hand.

His experience goes back over most of his sixty four years; starting as an apprentice fitter with Cammel Laird at Saunders Row and the technical college in Bangor, he has the natural grounding. He first got the stickmaking bug as a youngster, seeing demonstrations at shows and

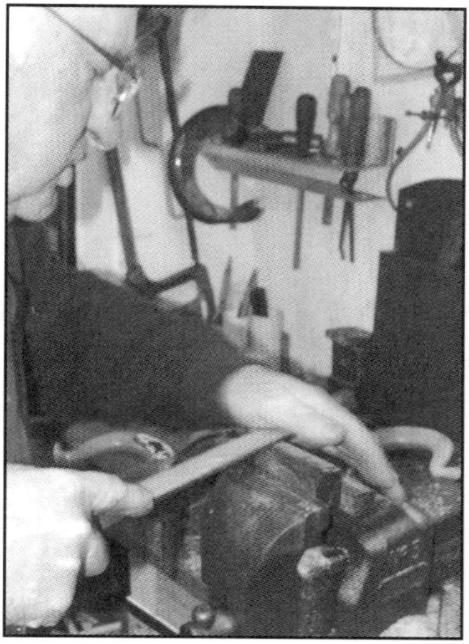

*Filing the horn*

*Len with a selection of his fine work*

thinking he'd have a go at it himself, then swotting up what he could from books. The enthusiasm at full throttle is still there.

Other senior members are happy enough simply in deep discussion and chat encouraging the 'novices'. And as you'd expect there's humour and banter there too.

As a leading club they sponsor stickmaking competitions and demonstrations throughout the region's agricultural shows, ploughing matches and sheepdog trials. In essence they are promoting a skill which is akin to artwork of the highest order. At best the exquisite stick handles painstakingly crafted from various animal horns are little short of creative magic. Animal and bird figurines sculpted and painted true to real life. At their benches at Glynllifon the club members aspire to this standard of excellence. In a sense it's this challenge that drives them on. Even Len whose right up there with the best says: 'I keep on learning something new each time I come here'.

Back home in Penisa'r-waen near Llyn Padarn and Peris, the Snowdon lake district, Len Porter is in his element greeted avidly by his wife Carol and the boisterous Begw. Begw almost dances a jig believing that Len will take her walkies. After his day at the hospitals, mostly

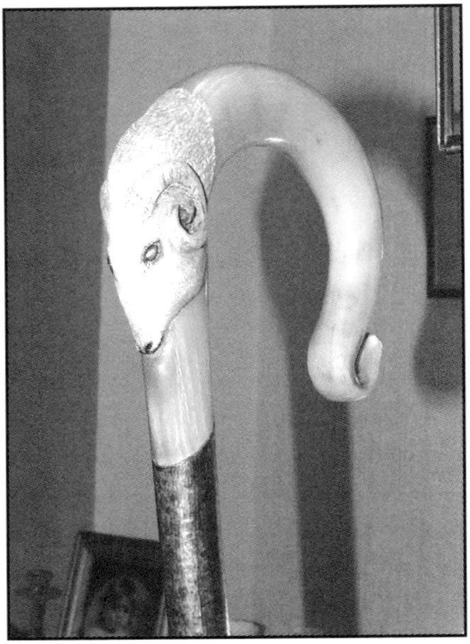

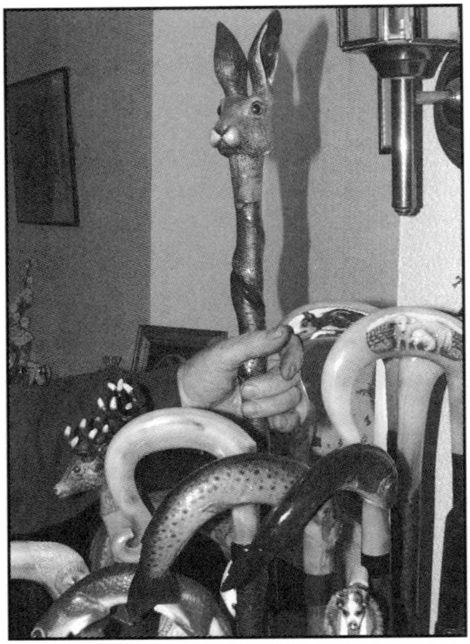

*Examples of Len's skill – and imagination!*

indoors, there's nothing he likes better than a country walk. He'll meet his mates, Begw loves to chase the grey squirrels, catches quite a few too. She's also a good ratter, he says. He has his favourite places where he can size up potential shafts. He likes hazel with its varied bark colour, the more attractive growing on the harsher ground. Sometimes if he sees a cluster of saplings, he'll cut some away so that one or two of the main ones get more nurture and grow on all the better. November and December is the best time to cut sticks, he reckons – well before they've started sprouting. But the winters are getting milder and the dormant period is getting shorter, he muses.

Back in the living room there's more stick interest. Scores of examples of his artistry with handles of various hues: many gleaming like ebony, which he explains are made from Indian buffalo horn. He has a friend who imports them by the truckload. Len would love to get buffalo horn of a lighter colour which have interesting designs on them, but they are getting very scarce due to the Japanese demand for them to make buttons. He clearly likes buffalo horn, not least for the wonderful depth of finish he can achieve with it.

He reaches for more sticks to show what can be done: the art work in handles knows no bounds given the imagination and skill of the true artisan. The head of a Welsh Black bull Deiniolen Dewi, which belonged to his neighbour and won scores of major prizes, is captured for posterity at the top of a hawthorn cane. The detail is incredible down to the ring in its nose!

Even Begw has her moment of glory emerging from a thumb stick worked out of a section of a deer's antler. Minute the little terrier may be, but all to scale instantly recognizable true to the mischievous eyes and the white and deep tan of its coat. It's a fable of country life, out of the other spur on the stick Len has worked a whistle to call her to order.

Another work of sheer genius is that of a wild salmon leaping out of a blackthorn rod, again the attention to detail is beyond belief the gills and the swirl of a fish in flight are all there. How does he do this lifelike image? Len is nothing if not inventive. One of the cleaning ladies in the Gwynedd hospitals where he works was clearing out some old magazines in the clinic waiting rooms, when Len saw a copy of *Trout and Salmon*, with exactly the picture he wanted there on the front cover. That's how he caught his salmon! It was then that Len the draftsman cuts in, he makes it all sound so simple with a felt tipped pen, he drew the magazine picture on to the horn. Then got to work with small chisels and drills. 'I have plenty of chisels, he says, this boxful was bought in a car-boot sale for a pound. While the even finer detail is done with obsolete dental drills thrown out having finished their shelf life at the hospital.' With Len nothing is wasted he can put almost anything to good use.

Always there's the attention to detail, for him its ever the quest for perfection. A good example of that is the curlew handled stick which he brings out, an exact replica of the real thing. He explains how on a field walk in the country he came across a buzzard attacking and killing a curlew. As Len ran across, the predator bird flew off leaving its prey ,whereupon he took his knife and cut its head off. He then quickly took it to the kitchen and popped it in the freezer. The curlew's head became available then as a precise pattern for when he came to fashion the handle. So the handle down to the feather formation, colour and even the length and curve of the long beak is a hundred per cent accurate. The eyes too stand out because a curlew has to look around, clear varnish provides for Len that necessary lifelike glisten.

All this of course comes about in the comparative later stages of stickmaking, after Len has shaped the horn into the semblance of a

*A raw ram's horn which needs to be straightened*

handle. Cyt one, the tiny workshop at the back of his home, is the power-house where it all happens. Apart from his stock of horns, from those of wild Snowdon Goats, Scotch Blackface sheep to Welsh Mountain rams and Indian Buffalo, his cyt is crammed full of tools and equipment.

It's apparent that the buffalo and the Welsh Mountain ram horns are the ones that he favours. The quality of the buffalo is consistently good solid throughout without any hollow parts but it's tough to work on. Welsh Ram horns of the quality he likes are not so easy to come by, his preference is for those of an older ram four years old at least. That usually means that the horn is mature and the walls are of a sufficient thickness. But he cautions that some ram's horns may have received heat treatment at some time in order to straighten them to appear well at shows or auction. Sometimes this will cause a flaw in the horn which will only be discovered when Len has already done a lot of work on it. In which case he'd have to start all over again with a different horn.

Len reaches out for a buffalo horn to show the processes he needs to apply. First he draws on it with a felt tipped pen to indicate a fairly long neck, which is where ultimately the stick will join up with the handle. Then as far as is possible, he will draw the remainder. These are the lines he will follow with his band saw, cutting the horn into its general shape. Having done that, further shaping is done using a special-purpose rasp. Although the rasp is highly effective, Len emphasizes the need to cut as much as is possible with the electric band saw. Next he puts the horn in a large pan of water to heat up and boil for at least half an hour.

While this is going on Len will get out a special jig and template which he made himself. It's based on one he saw some where on his travels, liked the idea and strengthened and adapted it to his own needs. To Len a professional fitter and time served welder this was no problem. Essentially by a system of ratcheting around a selected template, the horn can be moulded into shape. So boiling done, the buffalo horn is brought on to the jig for shaping and the process begins. Bit by bit the pressure is gently applied. Further heat may be needed and applied via a hot air gun (paint stripper) according to fine judgment. 'This should always be aimed at the inside of the curve or bend,' says Len, 'otherwise the horn will crack.' And the principal of leaving it tightly held in the jig overnight to cool down must be strictly observed else it will quickly revert to its old shape.

The processes from now on are the same as outlined in the previous chapter, but the means of getting there may vary! Len uses several ways to achieve his objective but the general principals must always be observed: in this the hot air gun is evident, as are the templates, and the applicator of precise pressure through a special jig which incorporates a small hydraulic jack (another of his creations). In all precision is paramount. When it comes to squaring the stick into the horn he leaves nothing to chance, the fit has to be perfect. His patience is boundless, a soft lead pencil marks the wood to show where a hair's breadth shaving may be necessary. The chisels he uses for any adjustment are not just sharp, they're razor sharp!

Len favours using a five inch masonry nail down into the dowel and the shaft to give the finished stick extra strength; this requires still more precision to ensure a hole true into the centre of the shaft to accommodate the nail. Again Len, ever inventive, has put together a tool incorporating a power drill to do just that .

The compound used to make sure that when the handle and the shaft are fitted together to be completely firm, is called Araldite; it comes in two tubes which when mixed together makes an extremely tight bonding.

Broadly the ram's horns receive the same treatment. 'They should be kept in an airy corner of the cyt to dry out and mature before the boiling to ensure a degree of subtlety in the handle formation,' he says. The need for a three inch neck to accept the shaft is also similar, as is the care to equate the bore of the horn to that of the stick. But, in so doing, clearing the hole in the horn adequately, of course, to accept the prepared shaft.

In all he does there's the attention to detail, the seven year Cammel Laird apprenticeship at Beaumaris learning alongside skilled time served craftsmen was time well spent. 'I enjoyed every minute of that,' he says. Now that skill, honed to perfection in the ancient country craft of stickmaking, is being passed on and the relay torch is held proudly aloft. What a great experience for the North Wales Stickmakers to have such a genius as Len Porter!

## Key points:

*Keep your tools in fine order and razor sharp.*

*Len Porter sharpens up with an electric twin grinder/buffer wheel, the latter is also ideal with car polish to shine up the finished handles.*

*Boil the ram horn for half an hour, longer for buffalo horn, in order to make it more malleable. Then place in a vice or jig to get it into shape handle fashion. Having done that leave it to cool overnight before releasing otherwise it will return to its original form. Do not boil it a second time, but a hot air gun (paint stripper) can be used to aid with the shaping. The hot air should always be applied to the inside of the curve otherwise cracking will occur.*

*Select your sticks during November December before they have started sprouting the dormant period. They should then be left to mature for at least a year in an airy shed or garage before starting to work on them.*

# Reasons for joining a stickmakers club

*Members of the North Wales Stickmakers and Llysfasi Stickmakers explain why joining a club is such a special experience.*
*Stickmaking appeals to men and women of all ages: members range from ten years old to over eighty – and they keep on learning something new.*

Most clubs now acknowledge their debt to R. G. Jones (Bob Gruff). In his day he was the king; pioneering the principals of stickmaking. His tools lacked the sophistication of the modern craftsman, relying on the basic blocks of wood for a template and the tools inherited from his father. Yet the work of this up country shepherd and farm manager, brought up in Llangwm in northern Wales, was of the finest. A Bob Gruff stick is still the standard by which others are judged.

Ray Jones secretary of the North Wales Stickmakers who workaday is in charge of loading and maintenance at Penmaenmawr Quarry readily admits as much. 'I owe a lot to Bob Gruff, he was the pioneer,' he says.

*R. G. Jones – Bob Gruff – king of stickmakers in his day*

'We now know how to squeeze the horn.'

'Here in the club we've built on what he taught us. There are many of us here, professional fitters and welders, who have made special jigs to do the work. And we're continuously adding new devices.'

Ray first joined the club in 1994 as a result of an item he'd seen in the *Daily Post* appealing for new members. The meetings at that time were held in a chapel vestry in Port Dinorwig and all that went on was talking and rowing, 'It was thoroughly boring,' he says. Then a few years later in an Anglesey Craft Fair they met up with people from Glynllifon College which led to a discussion with Eirwyn Edwards and an agreement to rent the workshop premises for four hours, once a month. This proved an excellent arrangement for the club, which has seen the membership grow to its present 120. There they use the student workbenches and when necessary bolt on additional vices.

The membership is still on the up! Anwen Harman from nearby Carmel, a Special Needs Teacher at the College, joined after a stewarding stint at the Caernarfon Show in 2005. She saw the club's exhibition and demonstration and spoke to Ray: result, she persuaded her husband Eddie and daughters Fflur ten and fourteen year old Llio to join. Already

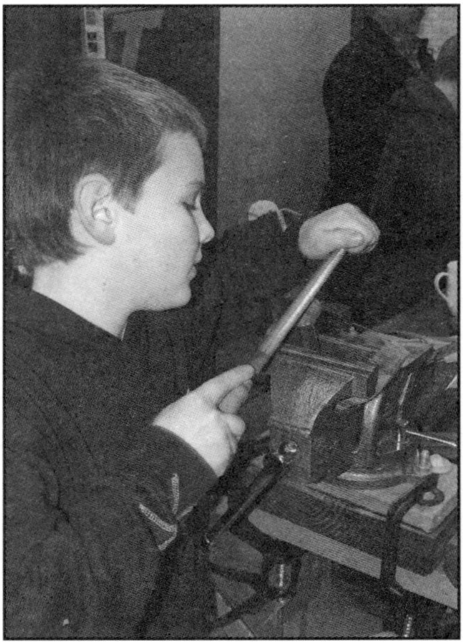

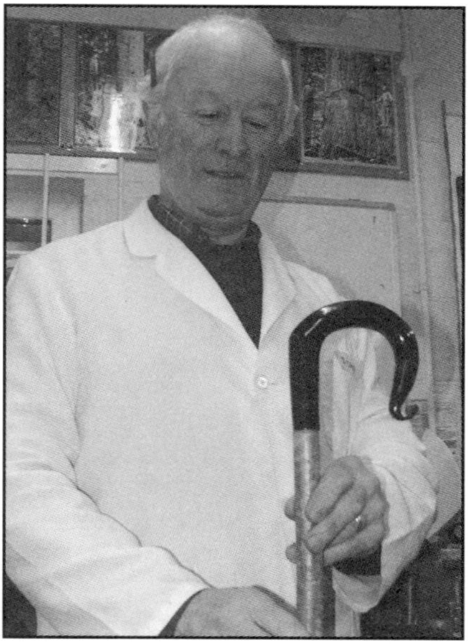

*Stickmaking appeals to all ages*

Fflur has won a cup for her stick in the junior section at the local show, which gained her points with her Brownie group. As well as being the centre of admiration when she showed her achievement in the chapel Sunday school. And Mrs Harman is abuzz with enthusiasm, so much so she's been elected the club's treasurer! While husband Eddie is doing what he always fancied having a go at. 'Everybody here is so helpful,' she adds.

Mel Morris a time served fitter-welder from Caernafon joined after seeing Bob Gruff demonstrating his craft on television, and thinking I'd like to do that. He then saw an item in the local paper appealing for new members to join the North Wales Stickmakers and responded. 'The club at that time was on the point of closing down,' he says. But since those days in the early nineties he's seen a dramatic rise in interest, particularly since relocating at Glynllifon. Over the years Mel has done everything and at the last annual general meeting finally gave up his role as membership secretary and tea maker! 'That will give me more time to do the sticks,' he says. But fifty four year old Mel will still be on hand to advise and encourage his mates. Pooling of ideas and experience is an important factor here. 'This is how the craft of stickmaking will carry on,'

*Members discuss and learn from each other*

he reckons, 'passing the skills on will ensure its survival to coming generations.'

Part of the club's future may well lie ultimately with eager beavers like fourteen year old Gareth Pierce and his brother Maredydd who is ten, from Tŷ Mawr, Ysbyty Ifan. 'We have a vice and things at home on the farm,' says Maredydd, 'and since we keep sheep we have a good supply of ram's horns. The older members show us here how to do the sticks, then when we get home we carry on till next time. Mel comments, the youngsters take it all in like a sponge and their work often puts the more experienced members to shame.'

Joseph Williams a sixty six year old plasterer from Caernarfon joined the club after attending an open day, two years ago at Glynllifon. And already he's notched up forty sticks! Like many of his mates he will find potential material while on country walks during the winter more or less, when the trees have shed their leaves. 'I keep my eyes glued for any bits of hardwood, I go round the rubbish skips and find plenty of stuff among what people have thrown out,' he says. 'Honest to God, what I find is priceles. The whole thing has enriched his life. I've learned so much about nature and farming through my involvement with sticks and it gets me

*Members of a stickmakers club concentrating on their work*

out of the house.' He's probably learnt a thing or two about human nature too because everyone here is always ready to share their knowledge. And good old style bartering is alive and well on a completely informal basis!

Dave Holroyd's interest, a club member since four years, is slightly different. Because although his day job is in plant hire, servicing machinery, his fascination is in wood carving. His current speciality is frogs, they dominate his home at Rhos Isa two miles down the road. And he has a field with a pond which is also full of frogs! 'You might say that I have an affinity with them.' So they adorn his stick handles! 'Anyone can put a handle on a stick, the trick is to put it on straight,' he says. He enjoys the competitions as well. 'I learn from them and strive to improve. It gets me round the shows and I'm renewing acquaintances all the time.' It was at an agricultural show that sixty three years old Dave first got his baptismal. 'Sticks are nice to walk with and for poking or pushing nettles out of the way,' he says.

Dick Price from Garndolbenmaen is living proof that your never to old to take up a new pastime. Seventy four year old Mr Price came in just over a year ago, a complete novice. 'For the first month or so I just came watched and listened. Then a member gave me a suitable piece of

*Andrew Jones explains a point at the Gelli Aur class*

hardwood, another produced a shank, everyone was incredibly helpful. I enjoyed it immensely and my interest grew. When your really interested you soon pick things up, all you need to do is to listen and look at how the other members are doing.'

Cledwyn Parry a seventy six year old retired butcher from Rhosgadfan is a stalwart member, here since the vestry days at Portdinorwic. 'I've always been interested in sticks, as a kid going for a walk after chapel I'd always have one in my hand that I'd cut and trimmed,' he says. 'You learn from your own mistakes; and surprisingly you keep getting new ideas to perfect your craft.'

Over in the Vale of Clwyd, the Llysfasi Stickmakers, the other northern Wales club, have their monthly four hour session in the College workshop. Here with a preponderance of skillful woodcarvers as members, the emphasis is slightly different. This means that many here take pride in their wooden handled sticks, and delight in their ability to work wonders with what they find in the most unlikely places. Frank Beddoe, who started stickmaking as a therapy after his heart attack seven years ago, shows a model dog made of American Cherry wood which he cut out of an old window sill that he found in a builder's rubbish skip.

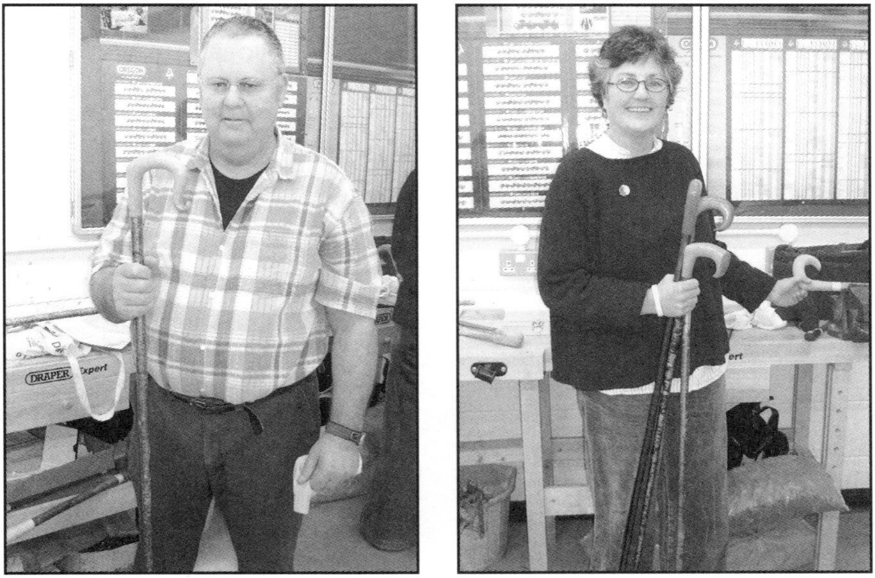


*Stickmaking appeals to both men and women*

Linseed oiled and varnished, it will end up as an ornate part of a novelty thumb-stick. Frank who comes from Shrewsbury says 'I don't like throwing anything away.'

Seventy three years old Peter Finch from Ruthin, a retired coach mechanic with Pentre Motors, has a similar tale. A friend brought him an old elm draining board: cut up and carved he wants to make a tractor to go on top of a stick with bits of it. With the rest he'll make a sheep's head and cut out toys for the kids.

Roger Bunn, the club's workshop manager and general factotum, is a founder member and happily makes the journey here each month from his home at Neston on the Wirral a distance of thirty miles. 'I've made sticks since I was a boy,' he says 'but not to my present standard.' Now he gives a lot of advice, especially on horn bending. 'It's easy,' he says 'because we have all the equipment here in the cupboard to do it with. The horn would be treated, and the member will take it home to work on. Then I advise them on what to do next! Horn is my favourite,' he says 'it's traditional isn't it.' His enthusiasm is infectious. 'It's worthwhile coming here, I'm usually here to open up and put the kettle on,' he grins.

Ken Williams who comes from Borras near Wrexham is the group's treasurer, which is appropriate given his forty years career in banking. His

*The Gelli Aur stickmakers' class*

interest in stickmaking goes back many years. But it was a bank client who first got him seriously involved. 'This gentleman suffered from Parkinsons Disease,' Ken explains, 'yet he was able to carve the most beautiful wooden handles. Surprisingly his hands steadied when he handled a knife or chisel.' One day he brought a stick with a robin carved handle as a gift and one with a thrush for Ken's wife. This is what gave Ken the urge to have a go at it himself. So evening classes notably with Bob Williams the Llansannan based stickmaker, together with a long standing association with the Llysfasi Stickmakers has perfected Ken's artistry. He now delights in giving talks to WIs, Rotary and other organizations about his hobby donating his fee to deserving charities. At the group, apart from his ability to advise his mates, Ken is keen to have theme events at their Saturday sessions in Llysfasi. Such as concentrating on different aspects of the craft, straightening the shaft, for example.

Like all stickmaking clubs there's great camaraderie here: all keenly anxious to help and advise their mates. Dave Evans from Holywell, a carpet fitter by trade, is the club's tool sharpener. 'I sharpen knives for these guys here,' he says. 'I do it the old fashion way using a two sided dry stone, one being fine the other medium, which I bought in Mold market.' Then he does the final flourish with a very fine four-hundred grit emery cloth over leather, to polish it up. 'By the time I'm finished you'll be able to shave with it,' he says. 'You can't teach people what I've been doing for thirty years. I never use a grinding wheel it gets too hot and softens the steel.'

Bruce Cargill from Liverpool – 'I've lived there at the back of Aintree Racecourse for 19 years,' – is the club's champion stickmaker for 2006. 'I get on well with the Welsh lads,' says sixty year old former TA man Bruce, who 'talks sticks, makes sticks and has a good laugh. Sticks have to be straight as a billiard cue – it's no use having a crooked Harry Lauder stick in a competition,' he grins. 'Competition keeps standards high.'

Paul Pemberton from Dyserth joined the club seven years ago after attending Emyr Howatson's course at St Asaph. 'I now demonstrate at shows and teach people how to make sticks, as well as urge them to join Llysfasi Stickmakers,' he says. Although sixty seven year old Paul was a carpenter before injury pensioned him off, his stickmaking interests are varied being equally happy with any variety of horn as with wood. 'It's an excellent hobby it gets you out looking for shafts and horn. And it gets you into wood carving,' he says.

Neville Mole, formerly a Buckley businessman up to his retirement in 1986, is the club's competitions manager and demonstrations organizer. These include events at numerous local shows including Caerwys Agricultural Show, the two day country fair at Bodelwyddan Castle, the Denbigh Flower Show, Afon Wen Craft Centre and the Open Day at Llysfasi College. These are duties he's carried out since 2000 in addition to stewarding and judging stints.

The old saw about giving the Secretarial job to a busy person is true here too, because Ann Williams came along with her husband 72 year old retired farmer Don from Ellesmere, and got roped in. She's won rosettes with her sticks but she doesn't mind admitting that she isn't as passionate about them as the men are. She has quite a lot of other irons in the fire including needlework, WI and Church; 'I'm involved in all of those,' she says. 'Stickmaking needs a lot of patience to do and these men have plenty of that, it's just amazing. And the atmosphere is lovely, they're so generous in helping each other.'

'Members come from quite a large area and now number 42,' she says. 'The membership fee is £5 a year and I keep all the paperwork up to date.'

The South Wales Stickmakers was formed on the 5th of April 1986 at a meeting in the Welsh Folk Museum at St Fagan. The group continued meeting there until 1993, when it moved to Dare Valley Country Park, Aberdare where the meetings are still held four times a year. The membership is drawn from West, Mid, South and East Wales as well as the West of England and some from even further afield.

Membership is open to anyone, the aim of the group being to promote and foster the craft of stickmaking. The meetings consist of workshops, demonstrations and presentations, by both members and guest speakers, on stickmaking and related crafts. Advice and assistance is freely available to anyone interested in taking up the craft.

Meetings which are always held on Saturdays, starting at 10am and continuing into the afternoons after a lunch break, are normally advertised by radio presenter Roy Noble (who is a Patron of the group) on his morning programme.

## Key points about joining a Stickmakers Club

*Members are always helpful and ready to share their tips and experience. You are therefore learning by watching and listening, even if you join as a complete novice.*

*You soon gain enough confidence to tackle your first assignment knowing that you always have help and advice close at hand.*

*Over time you can see what tools you need, often they may be in your garden shed already! In any case they sometimes can be bought relatively cheaply in the most unexpected places!*

*Joining is quite low cost. At the North Wales Stickmakers a charge of £1.50 covers a four hour session once a month at the Glynllifon workshop. Which includes a copy of Y Fagl, an extremely useful bi-lingual quarterly journal which details the clubs events programme and contains helpful short articles on stickmaking. Your admission to a centre of unequalled camaraderie.*

*The annual membership fee for both the Llysfasi Stickmakers and South Wales Stickmakers is £5.*

*The secretary of North Wales Stickmakers is Ray Jones, 36, Upper Water Street, Penmaenmawr, Conwy, LL34 6PB Telephone:01492 622 079 who is also the editor of Y Fagl, their bi-lingual quarterly.*

*The secretary of Llysfasi Stickmakers is Mrs Ann Williams, The Ridge, Lyneal, Ellesmere, Shropshire.SY12 0LE. Telephone:01948 710 334*

*The organiser of the Gelli Aur Stickmakers is Esther Barrett, Coleg Sir Gâr, Gelli Aur Campus, Gelli Aur, Llandeilo SA32 8LR. Tel: 01554 748589; email: esther.barrett@colegsirgar.ac.uk*

*The secretary of South Wales Stickmakers is Trevor Kidner, 50 Carlton Crescent, Gwaun Miskin, Beddau, Pontypridd, Mid Glamorgan. CF38 2RS. Telephone 01443 205 289.*

# D. Andrew Jones – Maintaining a Stickmaking Tradition

*Andrew Jones is the author of a stickmakers manual and acknowledged by Coleg Sir Gâr at Gelli Aur as a tutor par excellence.*

David Andrew Jones says, 'It was my Uncle Jim who taught me the art of stickmaking, but I suppose that I must have had the inclination from the start'. Uncle Jim was James Andrew Jones. Andrew is a family name going back several generations, 'most of them blacksmiths', he reflects. Uncle Jim was evidently a skillful country craftsman of the old school, marching in step with the eminent D.J.Davies of St Fagans Welsh Folk Museum. With their farming links they both remembered the traditional ways of doing things. Sticks were used by the Welsh drovers walking their livestock to the London markets. Baskets too, strongly framed, also had a multiplicity of uses around the farmstead. Wooden lovespoons and soup ladles crafted with simple tools were part of the old way of life.

Uncle Jim passed on these skills to Andrew Jones, so that preserved, they could be passed on to a rising generation. Andrew Jones is now acknowledged as the expert, often called upon to judge or instruct in the art of stickmaking. The courses he has conducted in Gelli Aur Agricultural College at Llandeilo have produced Wales leading exponents of the art. The courses are normally run on Saturdays from 10 a.m. to 3 p.m. – five hour sessions totaling twenty when completed. During a course, students will have produced two market sticks and two 'Sir Aberteifi' (Ceredigion) walking sticks, the latter being his speciality – uniquely his own. Now he proudly claims that over 80 people have attended and completed his courses.

A surprising offshoot of this resulted in one of his pupils, Clive George an office worker from Cardiff, approaching him with a proposal that together they should write a course manual of instruction on stickmaking. This resulted in 1998 in what many people regard as the stickmaker's bible, *Stick Making – A Complete Course* by Andrew Jones and Clive George, which to date has gone into nine reprints with a further updated edition due for publication at the end of 2007.

So what is Andrew Jones preferred raw material? For the shaft he likes hazel, particularly when found growing on river banks, because they are likely to have impressive mottled barks. He also likes blackthorn for the knobbly shaft which gives it a stylish image.

As for handles his first preference is for wood, 'There's a certain beauty about it,' he says. To prove his point he reaches for a stick with a beech handle on which he has carved the most exquisite horse's head, the mane lies lightly on the side of its neck, its jawbone giving it a spirited character. Andrew has an artist's eye with wood and enjoys the challenge. Does he need to have a picture or model to produce work of such refinement? 'No, I've seen enough of them during my lifetime as a farmer. Once I've seen something, I can remember it down to the finest detail.'

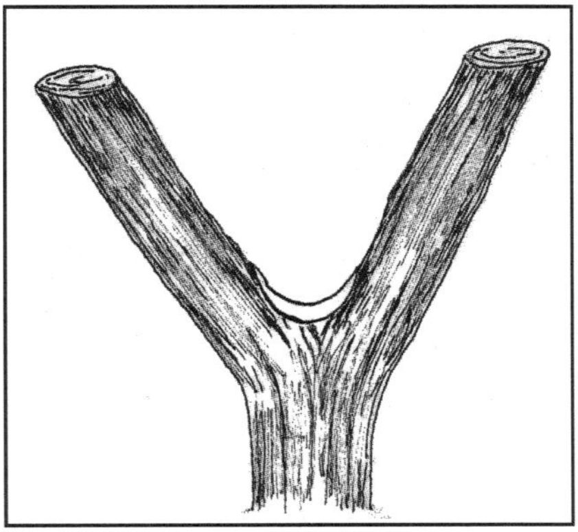

*The pit of the 'V' has been carved out for widening*

He then reaches for a stick with a handle on which he has carved a trout, so realistic that you expect its tail fin to swish as it prepares to leap. It's just another fine example of Andrew's creative skill with a rough piece of sycamore and the requisite tools : sharp knives, chisels and a band saw. The finished article is a work of pure genius. And what about the colouring? 'That's easy, I use aerosol car spray – four different colours

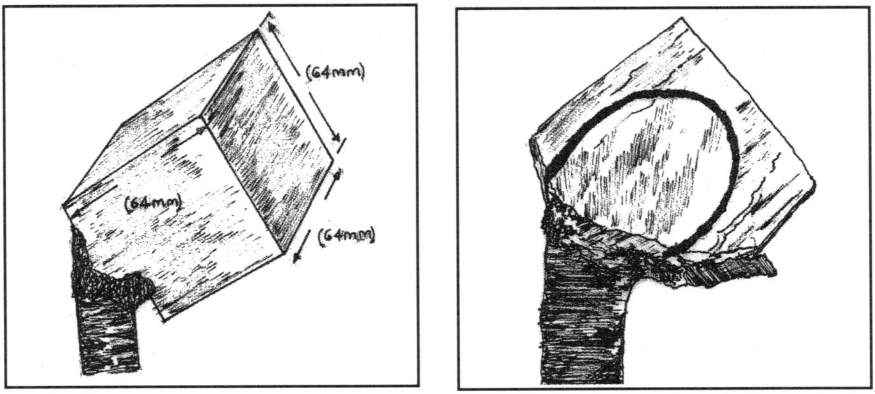


*A 'one'piece' stick and handle*

does the trick, then I dot the final spots on with a pointed stick. After that I apply the varnish', he says.

Andrew retired from farming 170 acre Pentre Sion at Pentre Bach near Lampeter, where he kept milking cows and fattened bullocks, in 1998. He now lives at Cwm Gwyn, a house that's built on land he once farmed. But he's not a man to sit around. His garden of about half an acre is a delight to the eye and grows a large variety of vegetables for the house. In the bottom corner he has his workshop with sticks in various stages of development. It's evident that he enjoys working with wood 'I like the feel of it' he says. Another example of his delight with wood are his wooden soup ladles made of sycamore or apple wood destined to eke out a measured portion. Again band saw, gouging knife, and a 'micro plane' in his artistic hands work their magic.

Elsewhere there is evidence of his skill with horn: cow's horn, Welsh rams, goats and buffalo and all the apparatus to shape them with formers. After all it's as a master stickmaker that his name is known the world over. He gets strange requests, non stranger than a call from America asking for an eight foot shepherd's crook for a show. 'I thought at first that someone was puling my leg' he says. Then later he got confirmation from one Jim Blumenfald. Yes, they wanted an eight foot shepherds crook, but not as Andrew thought for a farm show 'with animals and things', but for an operatic show to be staged on Broadway called 'Moses and Aaron'! He sent it there in two parts like a snooker cue extension, to be screwed back together on arrival at its destination.

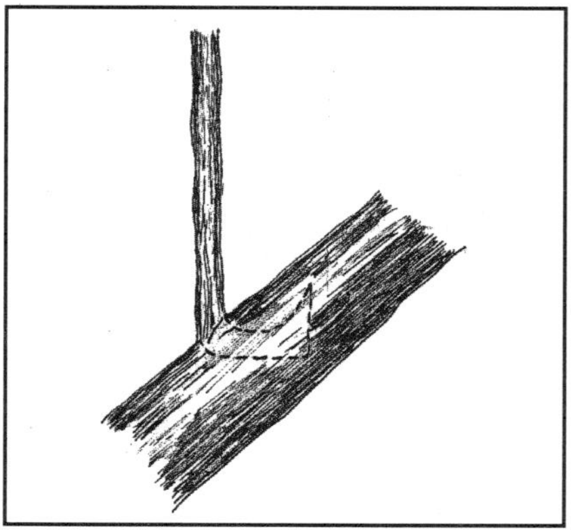

*A shaft growing at the correct angle to offer a 'Sir Aberteifi' stick to Andrew*

D. Andrew Jones, a leading authority on stickmaking and co-author of *Stick Making – A Complete Course* with Clive George is at Cwm Gwyn, Ffordd Llanwnnen Llanbedr Pont Steffan. Tel: 01570 422 629.

# Dafydd Davies, Master Stickmaker

*Want anything to help you on your way? Look no further, Dafydd is your guru! From advice about tackling a tricky problem to tools and raw materials to get on with the job, he's only a telephone call away.*
*He's unique, make him your friend!*

Dafydd Davies has raised stickmaking to the higher echelons of art form. In his workshop cum warehouse at Llanddewi Brefi in central Wales you will see evidence of his artistry. Dafydd's favoured medium for stick handles is ram's horn, and what he will show you will surely knock you over for their realism. Pheasants, Golden Eagles, trout they really live! From the colours, beaks and the piercing eyes of the birds to the fish, its tail a-swish, its mouth searching for bait and the scales still moist. That's a measure of Dafydd's achievement.

And he's only a village lad, born of every day mountain farming stock, spiced with wheel wrighting. His brother still farms at the homestead Aber-dau-ddwr, two and a half miles outside the village near the source of the Brefi, a tributary of the Teifi river. At busy lambing time

*Dafydd Davies – stickmaker's friend*

and haymaking Dafydd will be happily there lending a hand.

But his day-job is stickmaking which he came into after an apprenticeship in carpentry and furniture-making when he specialized in Welsh Dressers and Corner cupboards. It was a better cash flow prospect which induced him to change tack twenty years ago and take up stickmaking, a pastime in which he'd always had more than a passing interest. Then meeting up with Andrew Jones, the arch-druid of stickmaking at Lampeter nine miles away, to do a two year part time course of training. Dafydd was on his way. It was a brave move blessed with good fortune. Because he then met Gordon Flintoft, a mountain shepherd from Glaisedale in North Yorkshire, a character with thirty five years experience in the art. And Dafydd, now thoroughly immersed in the concept, was able to soak up Gordon's extensive knowledge. Dafydd believes that the will to learn is vital in stickmaking and he still has bags of that! Gordon Flintoft readily admits as much, that even with his vast experience, he's still learning something new. Dafydd now advises any budding stickmaker to keep on asking questions of the experts; 'you'll be surprised how readily they'll give you the benefit of their experience'. That's how it was when he went to meet Bob Gruff, the acknowledged northern Wales pioneer of the art, at his home in Abergele. Not only learning about hazel and horn but also the sculpting skill and artistry which went into Bob's creations.

And so he found the niche. By immersing in the experience gleaned by others over scores of years, Dafydd, in a comparatively short time, was able to perfect the art. He is now probably the only one in Wales who depends on this for a living. His commissions guarantee him full time employment for the next eighteen months.

He enjoys the challenge of horn, 'that gives me immense pleasure', he says. 'The horn is working against you all the time, and your task is to break that restriction.'

'With horn you are dealing, as with wood, with a life force – a commodity which has a mind of its own. Determined to go back to its original shape: the wish to return to the curl – and each one is different. The challenge with horn is greater than with wood, and I like that.'

Dafydd's sticks are now the most collectable item that you'll ever own: people in the know beat a path to his door. The ultimate recognition came at the Royal Welsh Show in 1986 when he met His Royal Highness the Prince of Wales who saw an example of his work. This led to a call

*Bob Gruff lead the way with new ways of stickmaking*

from Michael Forset, the Prince's equerry, requesting six specially engraved sticks for members of the Royal family. And so his fame has spread. One recent commission he's particularly proud of is the one he made for Archbishop of Canterbury Rowan Williams.

Remarkably at the workshop-power house in the centre of Llanddewi Brefi, his is still a one-man operation. Yet calls for speaking and exhibition engagements are fulfilled in all parts of the United Kingdom! There are Stickmaking clubs in most English counties, he says. And in Wales there are two strong clubs, one in northern Wales which meets monthly at Glynllifon College and the South Wales Club which meets at the Dare Valley Country Park four times a year including a stick show in September., But this may simply be the tip of the iceberg in Wales, where many small village groups are known to exist in addition to the Llysfasi Stickmakers (who meet monthly at Llysfasi Agricultural College at Ruthin) and another expected to be formed soon in the south.

From that early decision to go it as a professional stickmaker, Dafydd has progressed to being the number one stop for anyone in need of advice. And he's also got a brisk business going for the stickmaker's paraphernalia. Shafts of all kinds ready for the do-it-yourselfer, to ram's

*Dafydd Davies' workshop and warehouse at Llanddewi Brefi*

and buffalo horns for the handles. And all the tools needed to do the job.

He can also provide a selection of wooden handles ready for fixing to the shaft, kiln dried down to 8-10% moisture content, essential now that most houses are centrally heated. Naturally dried handles are 15% at best and may crack in present home conditions, he reckons. His supply of ram's horns are sourced from abattoirs throughout Britain: not so easily obtained since B.S.E. and the Foot and Mouth Disease epidemic brought a crop of government regulations in train. Never the less he manages to get a steady supply. They are boiled for ten minutes on arrival in order to extract the inner core and then stored for a minimum of six months to dry out. The drying out needs to be done in a manner whereby the horns have plenty of air circulating around them, yet not on a concrete floor. Dafydd ingeniously achieves this by storing them in banana boxes. And they come in all sizes: he shows a massive four pounder which once belonged to a seven year old Scottish Blackface and measures four foot in length when taped around the outside of the curl. 'Just imagine an animal carrying two of those on its head, that's what you'd call a real battering ram,' he says.

The buffalo horn are imported from India, Pakistan, China and

*Horn formers using a hydraulic jack.*

*Dafydd Davies with his sticks.*

Vietnam and come without an inner core, because although quite large weighing three and a half pound each, these are simply the tips and are relatively solid. He explains that there are two kinds of buffalo: the white skinned and the black. 'The horn of the white skinned come in various attractive colours: from gun-metal blue, Khaki brown to marble green some completely white. But currently they are extremely expensive,' he says, 'because they are in great demand by the Japanese who buy them to make buttons, while the Italians want them to make spectacle frames. The black skinned buffalo has black horn and is considerably cheaper and more easily obtained.' But for ingenuity Dafydd probably pips the wily Japanese, because not only do the black buffalo horns make excellent neo-marble finished handles, he can make shepherd's whistles out of them too! These provide the various tone pitches which trialists like and are also in demand by game shooters for calling their gun dogs. He has a customer from Holland, a market gardener who also trains sheepdogs over there. He regularly comes over to this country with a load of flowers and as the need arises nips over to see Dafydd and usually picks up an order of thirty whistles to take back with him.

## Key points

***Dafydd Davies – Wales, only full time stickmaker is at Fron Villa, Llanddewi Brefi, Tregaron. Ceredigion, Wales. SY25 6RS Phone 01974 298 566***

**For further study on stickmaking read:**

*Stick Making a complete course,* by Andrew Jones and Clive George. Published by Guild of Master Craftsman Publications ISBN 1861080832

*The Craft of Stickmaking,* by Len Gowan. Published by The Crowood Press. ISBN 186126375 9

*Further Useful Tips for Woodcarvers,* Published by Guild of Master Craftsman Publications Ltd. ISBN 1861081472

*Wildfowl Carving,* by Jim Pearce. Published by Guild of Master Craftsman Publications Ltd. ISBN 1861080085

*Power Tools for Woodcarving,* by David Tippey. Published by Guild of Master Craftsman Publications Ltd. ISBN 1861081049

## The British Stickmakers Guild

The Guild was formed in 1984 by a small group of stickmakers who felt that the many people practicing this old craft, usually entirely on their own, should be able to further their interest through a national organization. In the first year this small group had jumped to nearly 500 members – and continues to grow, now standing at 2000 including many from overseas.

Their main event in 1985 was the British National Stick Show which attracted an entry of over 350, an extremely successful opener. Currently the Guild runs the British and UK National Open Stickmaking Championship on a cumulative points basis, and stages some 30 shows up and down the country which counts in this championship. Its an event which culminates in the final National Show at Chatsworth in September each year. Various activities are held by local groups, all with the purpose of increasing personal contacts and in spreading the word about the craft.

The Guild publishes a quarterly magazine which is free to members, providing an information link between Stickmakers, Stickdressers and collectors. The whole spectrum of stickmaking is covered in articles from

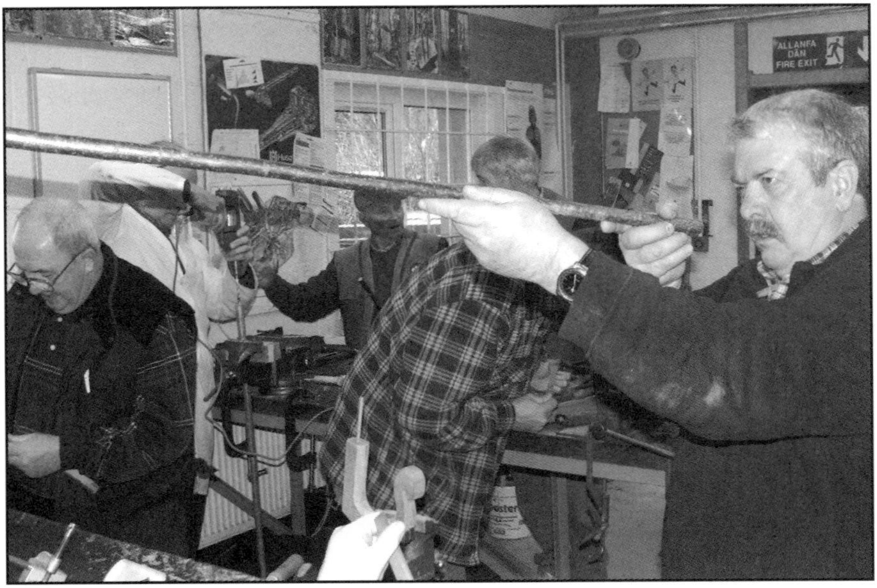


*A keen eye at Glynllifon*

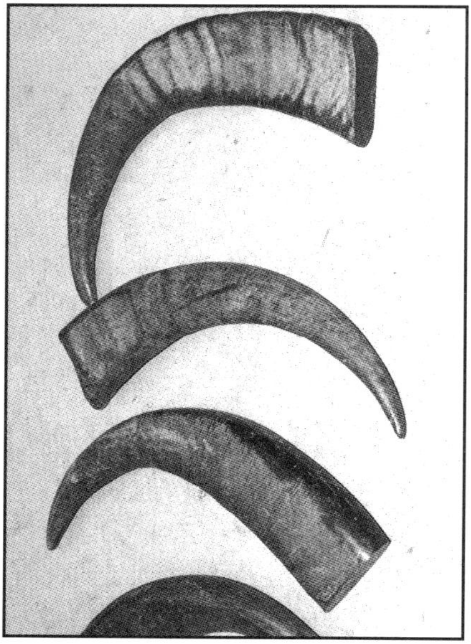

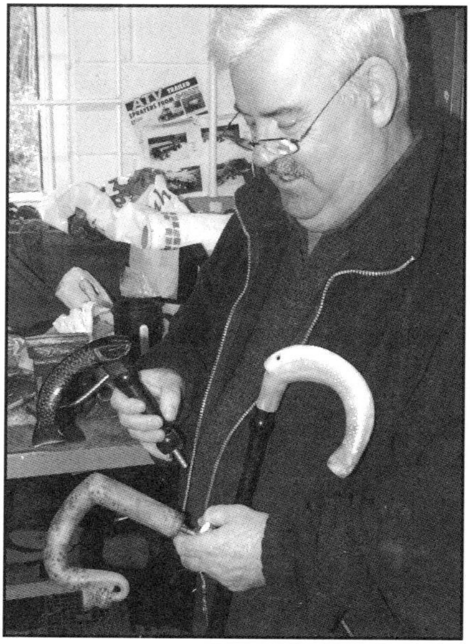

*From horns to finished handles – a sense of achievement.*

members, who share their knowledge, and delight in their achievements.

**The Secretary of the British Stickmakers' Guild** is:
Mr S. Clayton, BSG Membership Secretary, Grenfell, 32 Penistone Road, Hade Edge, Holmfirth, Yorks. HD9

# *Baskets*

## Baskets: A cause for nostalgia

*Baskets are part of a long heritage from the time of the Ancient Pharaohs to the present when they are favoured equally by balloonists cantering the skies, as by dreamers lolling in their wicker chairs. But in Wales, basket making as a skilled craft is in decline, a victim of cheap imports. All is not lost however – there are signs of a renewed interest a stirring in the willows!*

There's something very comforting about a basket. Fruit and vegetables, loaves of bread and cakes, are so much more appetizing when seen in a basket. Baskets are pure nostalgia. They represent all that is clean and wholesome. So much more than today's polythene-wrapped goods in a supermarket bag.

Baskets have a lot to be nostalgic about, they've been with us for

*An example of willow form baskets – the Welsh* cyntell

such a long time. From Moses, crib on the banks of the Nile, our first childhood story, baskets have held our affection. Throughout history, baskets have been part of our lives farmers used them to harvest their apples and potatoes. The butchers and bakers displayed their provisions. Fishermen caught their lobsters, as well as displayed their catch on greaseproof paper in them. Corves, made of coppiced hazel were used in the mines to haul the miners and the coal up. Even the weave of wattle within the walls of our homes relied on the basket maker's skills. Traveling trunks, hat boxes, umbrella holders and picnic baskets likewise. In a wicker chair we can lounge and dream our dreams.

All by British craftsmen, of native willow sturdy and strong, and made to last in a way that's unchanged for centuries. But alas we're talking of an industry in decline, truly professional basket makers are now very thin on the ground. The Worshipful Company of Basketmakers of the City of London was established in 1469 but by the time it received a Royal Charter from King George V1 in 1937 it was a profession on the wane, its responsibilities taken over by trade unions. Cheap imports from outside Europe using low paid labour took its toll. From 1945 to 1980 the numbers of traditional basket makers fell from 7000 down to 500, of whom 200 were in workshops for the blind. So we have to say that accomplished basket makers are now very few. Fortunately it's still possible to buy a traditionally hand made basket produced by time served Welsh craftsmen using home grown willows. The main natural growing areas in Wales being on the Gwent Levels, the Vale of Glamorgan, Anglesey and the wet lower flood plains of the main rivers. Cardiff University has trialed over 50 varieties of willows in coppices in Powys as commercial crops for craft, basketry, sculpture and floristry. But the main supplies still come from Somerset where for the last fifteen miles of its slow meandering course the River Parret is tidal, and during the winter months, often bursts its banks, inundating hundreds of acres of farm land. Growing best in thick loamy soil, on land that is sometimes flooded, but at other times well drained this is ideally suited for willow growing.

Or you can do it all yourself which this book urges you to do.

As with all crafts the best way to learn and become proficient is to join a course with a qualified practitioner. By featuring in this book a chapter on the methods employed by just such a person, Beryl Smith of

*Aeryn Owen Jones of Llangwm*
*displaying the various aspects of the hedge layer's craft*

*Professional hedgelayer Aeryn Owen Jones in action,*
*and below the finished hedge – Uwchaled style*

*Fimished hedges – central Wales style*
*with pleated hazel lengths along the top*

*Andrew Jones*
*with his one-piece hazel sticks and crooks*

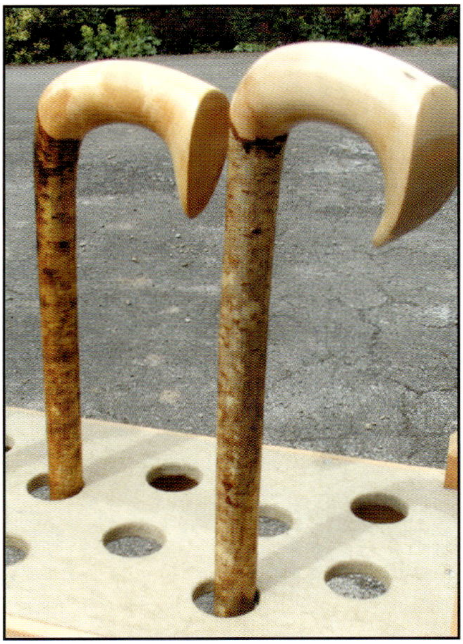

*Andrew in his workshop*

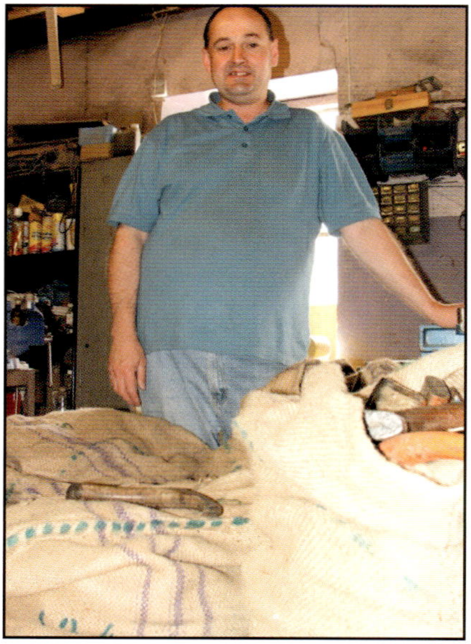

*Dafydd Davies*
*the only full-time stickmaker in Wales*

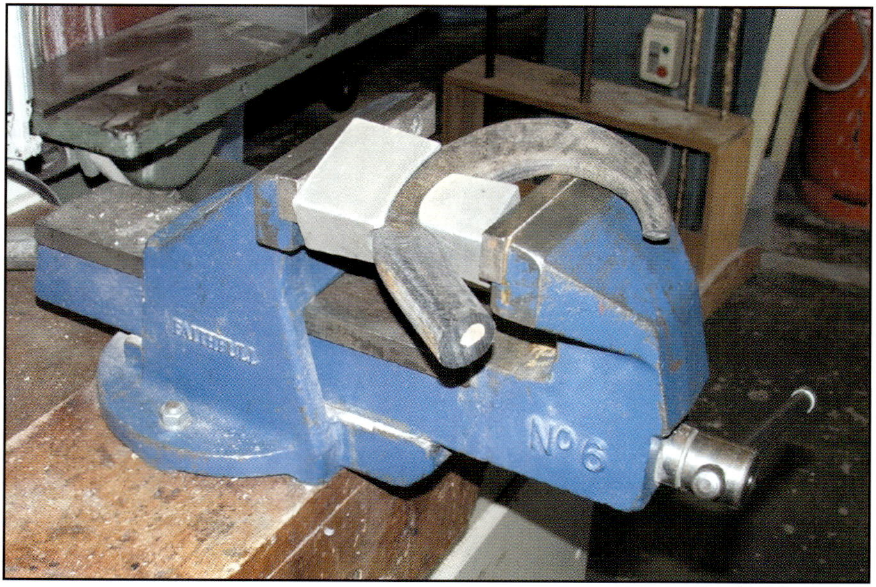

Stickmakers at Glynllifon near Caernarfon

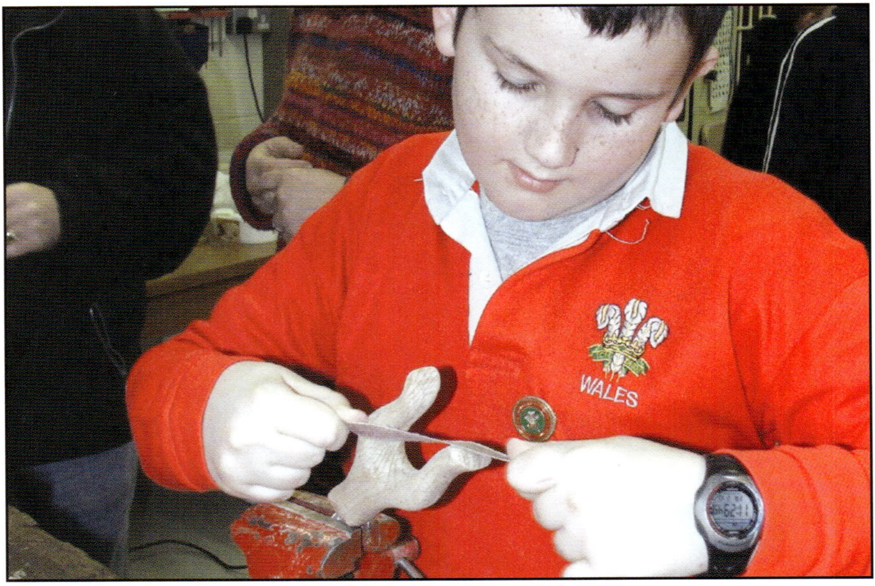

*Essentials of the craft:*
*horn, a selection of shafts, and below, a high tech device to shape horns.*

*A fine display of the carver's craft*

*Len Porter with his collections*

*A stickmaking competition at Sioe Nefyn*

*Llysfasi stickmakers*

*Marvin Morgan*
*with an example of his work*

*Ram horns*

*Stickmaking competition at the national Welsh Show at Llanelwedd*

*Marvin seen splitting the willow to create ribs for his* cyntell *– Welsh frame basket.*

*Creating a* cyntell *– step by step with Marvin Morgan – the main frame is formed around a bicycle wheel!*

*Stages in* cyntell *basketry*

*An exhibition of Welsh coppice grown willows at the Welsh Show*

Llanidloes in central Wales, it's hoped that you'll feel inspired to have a go.

Additionally there is an abundance of books and literature as well as the extremely instructive Coates Willows at Wetlands Centre at Meare Green Court, Stoke Saint Gregory, near Taunton to help you. Founded early in the nineteenth century this family run concern can supply all the needs of the basket maker, from the various willows and tools of the trade to a useful explanatory video show. Coates have received a well deserved tourism award and gained an enviable reputation as a visitor centre. It's a place to go to!

# J. Marvin Morgan –
# Authority on the Welsh *Cyntell* Basket

*A career at St Fagan led him to D.J.Davies , the acknowledged expert on Willow Framed Baskets, traditionally a Welsh* cyntell.

James Marvin Morgan was born in the coal mining village of Seven Sisters named after the pit owned by Evans and Bevan who had seven sisters, hence the name. The Welsh name is Blaen Dulais after the river Dulais , a tributary of the Neath which it joins ten miles further down the valley.
Marvin's recollections are of a childhood with a growing yen for country life, so that by the time he was fifteen his favourite pastime was going down to help a local farmer with his livestock. That began his resolve on leaving school to work with horses on a farm, a wish largely fulfilled when in 1949 he left Seven Sisters to go to Pen Fedw Farm near Moriston, Swansea. 'It was a 90 acre farm run solely on horse power,' he says. Even then it was rather unusual. Milking the cows was done by hand, lighting was with paraffin lamps or candles, 'everything was done the old

*Dry willlow*

*Basket forms*

*D. J. Davies at St Fagan's*

fashioned way'. Here he was taught a lot about rural crafts such as 'hedge laying and the other things which needed doing'.

'When I was at Pen Fedw part of my duties was to take corn to be ground at the White Mill down at the lower end of the hill', says Marvin. This was normally his Friday job, taking bags of oats and barley by horse and cart to be brought back from the mill in meal form for the farm animals. Part of the arrangement was that he would stay there for the day to help the miller to grind other people's corn as well. In exchange for this the Pen Fedw farmer had his corn ground 'for free'. In this way Marvin became conversant with the old style of milling: the gearing and dressing the mill-stones.

So finding himself between jobs in 1977 on a visit to St Fagan's Welsh Folk Museum, he discovered that there was a vacancy for a miller there. This seemed to be a job that was ready-made for him, so he filled in an application form and duly got on to the payroll at St Fagan's. Thus began a career which commenced in October 1977 and was to last for the best part of 20 years. Being the miller at Melin y Bontbren at St Fagan's brought him into contact with the doyen of country craft there, D.J. Davies, who was essentially the estates manager. Born in Caio in Carmarthen, 'DJ was a typical rural craftsman'. In the museum's early days Dr Iorwerth Peate had enrolled him there as a traditional basket maker, but being a farmer's son DJ soon also became a valued adviser in the development of the St Fagan's site. It was Marvin's good fortune to strike an immediate close friendship with him, fostered by their common interest in farming and country pursuits.

Stickmaking and traditional basketry were among the interests that they shared, DJ being an artisan in both. Thus under his wing the young Marvin's skills were perfected. At the museum craft fairs Marvin would demonstrate stickmaking while DJ would show frame basketry. At one such fair DJ told Marvin that this would be his last, he was then 82 and it was getting too much for him. Realizing the need to preserve his skills, Marvin and Les Llywelyn , a stickmaker at the museum, arranged with DJ that they would go to his workshop fortnightly for a thorough course of instruction. 'We did that for 12 months' says Marvin, 'during which we were taught the rudiments of doing a frame basket.'

Doing a traditional willow frame basket – in Welsh called a *cyntell* – is totally different to doing an ordinary basket claims Marvin. For example 'with a *cyntell* basket you need to split the willow, and put it over your knee and thin it down, so that it's flexible enough to make a rib'. Back in rural Carmarthenshire DJ had been taught by his grandfather in the ancient craft. Frame baskets were central to country life : they would be used in carrying a feed of chaff, pulped swedes and barley for the farm animals; at harvest time they were used to gather potatoes or the orchard fruits, equally the same kind of basket would be used by the women to take the washing to the clothes line, some were even used as a baby's cradle.

Marvin vividly recalls his first visit to DJ's workshop and being surprised to see, hanging on pegs behind the big door, bicycle wheels of various sizes from small to extra large. DJ explained, 'if you put a green

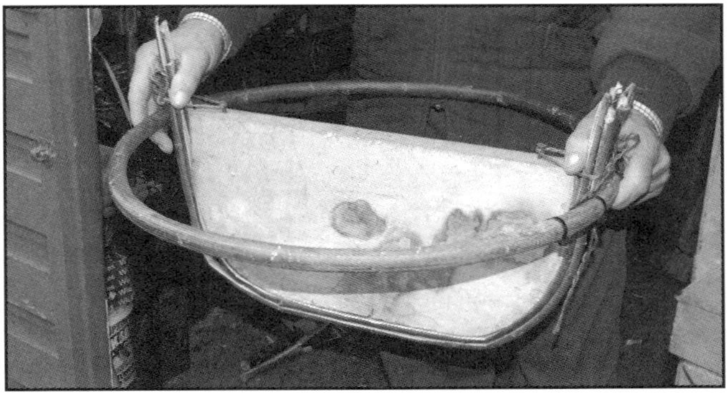

*The steps of making a* cyntell

willow around a bicycle wheel and leave it there, within a month it's seasoned and when it's taken off , there's a natural curve in it. It stays that shape and provides a circular neck for the basket.'

'I remember asking DJ, how did his grandfather manage before the bicycle wheel?' He replied: 'on corners of the farm buildings there were barrels which were used as water buts to catch the rain water coming off the roof; these were used as frames. When bikes came along, they saw a use for old bicycle wheels !'

During that year with DJ, Marvin was drilled in the art of splitting the green willow and taking the slithers away. The willow was an inch in diameter, often DJ would like to use a wild rose because the stem didn't taper.

The principals with baskets for shopping were broadly the same but the handles would be incorporated from the start.

Marvin has his own small willow nursery, much as his basketry ancestors may have had, but makes a concession to progress by also buying as needed from the Somerset Levels to introduce colour into his work. 'Years ago baskets would all be the one buff colour,' he says.

'Once I started basket making, I realised the simplicity of the tools. A knife, secateurs and loppers to cut the willow is all that's needed.'

# Beryl Smith Basket Maker

*Profile of a central Wales basket enthusiast: how she became addicted! She grows her own willows as well as buying from the Somerset Levels. Willows are undervalued they have varied sculpture uses, growing willow schemes as well as conventional shopping carriers, log baskets and willow coffins. Here she explains her methods*

'There's no wire, there's no glue, no nails just willow, that's all there is.' So says Beryl Smith, basket maker and willow artist of twenty five years standing at her workshop on the rarefied eleven hundred foot skyline high above Llanidloes in central Wales.

Here on clear days the view down towards Trefeglwys and across the Severn plain towards Shrewsbury is a glorious panorama. She moved here in the early eighties from Tewkesbury in Gloucestershire where she had a shop and was 'always fascinated by the baskets we used to have'. But, ever a practical sort of person, she had taken up weaving much earlier. So basketry was only a short remove from that. And that step was

*Basketry competition and craft display at the Welsh Show*

taken when she met an old basket maker who used to cut all his willows off the banks of the River Severn. I went along to meet him and just got inspired, she says.

It was the Tewkesbury experience which drove her on when she came to Wales, having met Sheila Winter who had been Tewkesbury taught in the art of basketry. And it was a two day course with Sheila that sealed her destiny! There was no looking back.

Beryl Smith is now very much in tune with her landscape at Goetref, Bwlch y Fan where its southerly aspect greets the morning sun and her workshop overlooks idyllic Powys. In her paddock behind the house, a boggy patch, she has her raw material, the willows growing. These are no ordinary willows because they are varieties selected for their distinctive colours. The Flanders Red, produces an orange stem while Hutchinson Yellow, gives a nice contrast. 'But there are hundreds of different varieties in the catalogues to choose from,' she says.

Harvesting the willows is carried out between November and March when the sap is low and the leaves fallen, the stems are then graded according to length. Beryl explains that the object of this is to have stems of the same length and thickness together: as they go up in length they get thicker, she says. She will leave the bark on, but the quantities that she buys in from Somerset will come ready stripped and are therefore smoother and more flexible.

Preparing for basket making needs a bit of forethought since the stems to be used will have to be well soaked in water: the stripped ones will have to be immersed in her water tank according to their length at a rate of an hour per foot, whereas the ones with bark on will require a day per foot longer in Winter, so you need to think ahead. On bringing them from the tank they are wrapped up to mellow, overnight and the basket making carried out while they are still moist. For a traditional shopping basket the base is worked using three medium thickness sticks with three more crossing in the middle for a small basket, or four by four for a much bigger one. This will provide the framework for pairing under-and-over using two rods. This is like feathering as lain on top of a new laid hedge is sometimes done, to form an upwardly concave bottom for the basket. For strength, the base is bent over the knee occasionally while being worked. The medium thickness side stakes will be spliced and inserted either side of the bottom stakes of the base to form the frame for the side of the basket. The thinner stems will then be woven circular fashion using traditional basket techniques, and here there's an opportunity to introduce colour if desired. The long stakes left after the sidewall is finished is laid down to form a border on the top edge of the basket, and the bow handle incorporated if desired.

Another of Beryl's favourites is the frame, fruit basket, in which she uses a hoop frame: dog rose makes a fantastic hoop and when dried and spliced is very strong likewise hazel or willow, she says. The hoop will form the main frame, then it's a matter of under-and-over weaving as with the basic shopping basket, adding ribs as you go to form the shape you want. She also makes willow coffins, using all of the traditional basketry techniques: these are a sustainable alternative to the conventional coffin and ideal for the green burial sites.

The management of the willow nursery is relatively straightforward: the ideal requirement being a fairly boggy piece of land (but willow can be grown anywhere), then it's simply a matter of pushing the stems into the ground during the winter and because its got all the hormones in the bark it needs, it will create its own roots. The roots will develop during the winter and, come the spring, they will be all ready to sprout and grow. The earlier in the winter that they are planted the better. They should be ready to be cut for harvesting in the following winter, by which time, since they are grown on stools, they will have grown three or four stems. The next year there might be eight or ten and by the fourth there will be twenty or thirty. 'It's an amazing plant and all the care that's needed is to keep the plantation free of weeds. It's very much underrated,' Beryl comments.

In terms of flexibilities of use the willow is almost boundless and, living as we do in an increasingly environment friendly age, its significance is becoming daily more apparent. Gardeners see the possibilities of living willow structures, not only in creating garden seats and sculptures, but also making use of its instant growing features for covered arches and avenues (due to its ability to strike roots so quickly). Part of Beryl's remit frequently takes her along these channels accepting commissions in London funded by European sources to create living play areas. Often these involve young people delighted to take part in a project, and learning the basic elements at the same time. She sites, as an example, how JCBs cleared the tarmac, while youngsters wheel-barrowed horse muck courtesy of the horse guards and covered that with top soil, before sticking the saplings in to produce an attractive arboretum and play area. 'By the finish it looked rather like a bomb site,' she says, 'yet in three weeks the willows were greening up and flourishing and two years later had become a green oasis.'

Willows can create wind breaks in gardens, or with their matted root formation are ideal in anti erosion schemes. Growing tunnels, outdoor classrooms, dens and amphitheatres excite children's imagination. In a Hull park a wonderful archway; over a serpentine path at Stourbridge an environmentally friendly garden feature: for Beryl it's all part of the commissions that come her way. She likes the flexibility of willow, a challenge to her imagination. She would dearly love to do a living willow maize: the prototype is there, all she needs is a commission.

So the willow in various guises has a range of possibilities: Beryl Smith mentions sculptures which are rapidly gaining in favour to adorn town squares and provide a focus of interest. Dragons, dolphins and eagles challenge the ingenuity of the willow devotee. One fine example of her work, a full sized seven foot wolf made from dried willow, can be seen in the wood near Tan y Bwlch which is staggeringly realistic when people see it from the Blaenau Ffestiniog train. This was commissioned by the Forestry Commission for locating in an ancient woodland claimed to be the last place in Wales to be inhabited by wolves.

But teaching classes and workshops, part of the weft and weave of her life, also take in rush-work. This grows on the banks of the River Avon in fast flowing water: it's not what people think of as the course bull rush but our own native bull rush which can be identified by its particular flower. She produces a straw hat, a typical example of her craft, which she made twenty years ago and still wears constantly in sunny weather. The same basic rules of basketry under and over – apply here too. But with rush it's floppy when wet so you have to make it over a mould. For this she uses an old oval biscuit tin with newspaper taped on, according to the size required, for her hat mould. 'You start with a square first of all then go down the hat mould, pairing and weaving as with baskets. I like working with rush because when it's wet it's like silk,' she says.

'The best way to learn weaving, basketry or living willow is by joining a class or workshop. Some I do from here in my workshop,' she says, 'others are done for Powys County Council at Trefeglwys and Llanidloes.' She has also done some for an organization called Glasu, a Leader 2 European funded project at Builth Wells but emphasizes that courses can be arranged anywhere in the U.K. and she has worked countrywide in schools on environmental projects. At beginners courses she goes slowly with everybody, making a small basket, sculpture or willow structure, and demonstrates every stage. 'Anyone who's used to working with their hands can usually pick it up very quickly,' she says. 'Traditionally basket making was a man's job, now the courses I run are mainly attended by women. But it's more of a leisure thing now isn't it. Whereas before, it was employment. With willow baskets being used extensively in the home, industry and horticulture for centuries, every village had its basket makers. This however took a sharp decline with the invention of plastic. Hopefully it will come full circle as we head for a more sustainable future.'

## Key Points

***Basket-maker Beryl Smith of Crafts Mid Wales who runs classes and workshops in Basket Making; Weaving; Spinning and Living Willow Sculptures is at Goetref, Bwlch y Fan, Llanidloes. Powys. SY18 6NS Tel. 01686 430 314***

***Willow the raw material for making baskets can be easily grown in any land but prefers a boggy patch. Simply stick a cutting in the ground in November and see how well it's grown by the Spring!***

***Willow must be soaked in a water tank and wrapped up to retain the moisture for work in successful basket making. Stripped willow for one hour per foot length of the throngs, that with the bark still on – for one day per foot.***

***Willow is the most versatile plant, equally good growing in garden schemes, as worked in sculpture creations and green coffins.***

***Baskets went out of fashion soon after the war when plastics took over. Now they're coming back. Many supermarkets now make a charge for plastic bags. Baskets are strong, light, re-useable and environmentally friendly.***

*Ken Griffiths at work on a conventional basket*

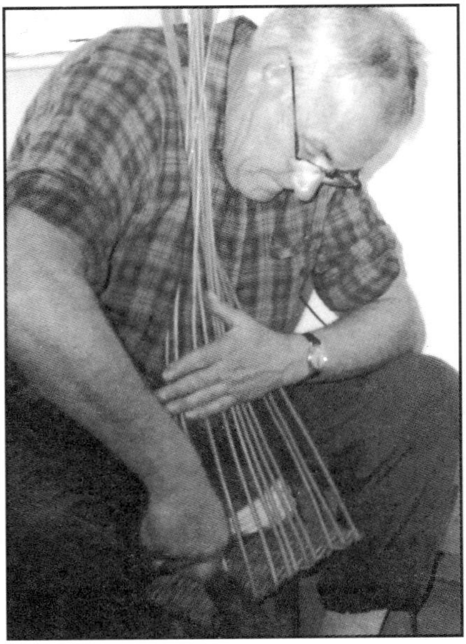

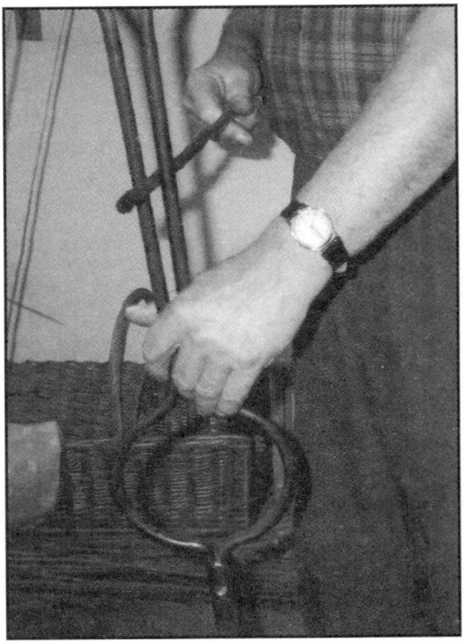

*Using a hand held device to strip willow*

# Ken the Basket Maker Remembers

*Willow growing in Bangor on Dee Harvesting the Willow a once communal event Stripping, drying and storing History of a business from Coracles to Motorbike Panniers! A continuing tradition.*

Ken remembers cutting willows which were nearly fifteen feet long on the Johnson's willow beds in Bangor on Dee when he was a lad. That was before the days when the authorities began using great big excavators and JCBs to excavate the ditches around the area. Years ago they cleared the ditches with a shovel to a depth of two feet to facilitate drainage, but now with these machines they go down to five foot. This means that the willow beds are a lot less marshy and the best we can now get is nine foot willows. Still, that isn't bad going when you consider that its only one season's growth.

The beds are on the banks of the Dee river, fairly boggy land which is covered with a crust of firm ground. It's near ideal for osier growing, which grows best in marshy land the wetter the better. But harvesting the willows can be tricky. Ken Griffiths recalls occasions when tractors have

*Ken Griffiths at the Johnson workshop at Bangor on Dee*

sunk towing a load home 'once the hard crust of top soil is broken you're in serious trouble,' he says. He remembers as many as three tractors in tandem having to get the load away. So experience has shown which is the safest way to go, and the weight to carry.

Cutting and stripping the willows is carried out in the Spring. In early April Ken will examine the crop, with his thumb-nail he'll check the quality of the bark and judge whether the sap has arisen sufficiently for it to peel. When that time has come, it's all hands on deck and there's not a moment to lose, harvesting has to be completed in five weeks Ken and Robert and Paul Johnson will drop everything and make their way a quarter mile down the road to the willows, armed with hooks to cut the crop. The routine then is to cut the willow, clean off the whiskery shoots and lay them into three rucks according to their length large, medium and small.

They are then carted back to the workshop where the willows are stripped that is the bark is removed by a break, which is driven by an electric motor. This is quite a far remove from the days when the work was done manually, almost as a communal event by ladies from the village. Ken well remembers those days when the women would be alerted and taken down in a van. They'd been doing this for years there was Mrs Barlow, Jessie Pollitt, Hugh and Charlie's missus and Ma (Ken's mother) who just wouldn't miss it for the world. There would be about nine in all and their day began, tying in with their domestic responsibilities, at 9.30 and finished at three.

'We then took the bundles for the girls, to peel, using the special tool known as a break,' Ken reflects. 'They would sit in a circle to do the work with great skill and precision and chat away, it was quite a communal event. But you'd be surprised, one would prefer to peel the large ones, another the medium or small – and they'd get really cross if they were given the wrong bundle. They'd shout, take them away, I want the big ones! The bundles were then tied up, danced level and stood up against the shed to dry much as they're done today. Then left out the following day, hopefully to get some sun and afterwards brought inside to lie over wire racks for further drying providing the white willow for baskets. But mechanized willow stripping nowadays has meant that the work can be done much quicker.'

The buff coloured willows were produced by retaining some unpeeled willows which were boiled in a large boiler, then peeled: it was the dye out of the skin that gave them their colour. At one time the custom was to boil them in urine a practice which has been long superceded! But the production of buff willows at Bangor no longer occurs since the company's decision to buy them in from elsewhere.

That's broadly the cycle of events which provides the material for basket making for J. Johnson and Son at Bangor on Dee. A concern which began one hundred and twenty years ago when James and Charlie Johnson, coracle salmon fishers on the River Dee, decided to diversify. They already made baskets and coracles from willows growing on the banks of the river to supplement a meager income. Coracle fishing was a very efficient way to catch fish and the authorities became concerned about the reduced stocks in the river, with the result that permits to fish became increasingly difficult to obtain. Times were hard for the brothers when this was imposed; James had six children, Charlie had twelve and basket making became their only means of survival .

One of James, sons also named James joined the army when he was eighteen and was seriously wounded in the 1914-18 war. At Beckitts Park Hospital in Leeds a bone was removed from his leg to repair his damaged left arm.

*A selection of tools used in basketry*

Part of the treatment to strengthen his arm was basket making. This enthused him in the craft and on leaving hospital he served a two year apprenticeship with a firm of basket makers in Leeds. Whilst in hospital he met a local girl Mabel Marion Arnold whom he married and brought back to Bangor on Dee. After working with his father he decided to plant a willow bed, rather than rely on the haphazard growths alongside the river. That was the nucleus of a family business which still flourishes; James, son Cyril continued the tradition, well drilled in basketry for forty years by his father, he became a true artisan. So Cyril the craftsman and his wife Jane considered to be the driving force, progressed the company. It is still very much a family business, their five children, three daughters and two sons, have all been trained in the craft, and two daughters and a son now work full time in the business. Cyril died in1997 and the company, firmly craft based on sound principles which he had set down, continues under the inspired leadership of his widow Jane. Due regard must be made of Ken's role too as a vital asset to the company.

What makes this story even more fascinating is that Ken has a direct family link because James, he of the severe Great War injuries, was also his Grand Dad. Indeed his recollections as a ten year old reverberate around the workshop and his grand father's tales of his apprenticeship years with a company which employed twenty basket makers who made very good money, working on a piece work basis, from nine o,clock until four thirty thanks to a particularly strong union. That was good experience for when he came back to Bangor on Dee and revitalized the Johnson business. When Cyril took up the mantle from his father, Ken's expertise grew alongside his kinsman. Those were the zenith days of basketry. Ken could have had no better mentor: working and learning alongside a great artisan.

That's Ken's life enjoying and raconteuring about a life with willows: remembering days when they sent big lorry loads of seasoned willow to Manchester or by train when Bangor had its own station and rail connection, prior to the Dr Beeching cuts in the early sixties. Those were the epic days before plastic and cheap imports took their toll. But within this family and village, the ancient skills are cherished. At Johnsons they respond to any basket request. The workshop behind their shop and showroom in Malpas Road is reminiscent of a bygone age, callers come to discuss their needs. A goose made of willow for a pantomime, at another time panniers for a motorbike. Another unusual one, a Bath Chair it's a family concern that certainly enjoy a challenge. On occasion the Duke of Westminster will call wanting small chairs; or sometimes a call for something special for Chirk Castle.

Ken will then go to the willow store and make his selection. The orders keep rolling in

The basket tradition is set fair for the future at Bangor on Dee a new work-shop cum showroom adjacent, in course of erection at the close of 2006, is earmarked for educational and demonstration purposes. Jane Johnson says this is what her late husband always wanted. It's Cyril's vision being fulfilled.

## Key points

***In modern willow beds the rods are cut as close as possible to ground level and there is very little to be seen after harvesting except a knotty lump underfoot. These beds are ideally suited to cutting by machines.***

***Cutting at ground level is known as coppicing, while cutting at higher levels as practiced at Bangor on Dee is called pollarding, the new shoots growing from stumps at a handy two foot from ground level.***

***When required for basket making white willows are soaked for one hour and allowed to mellow for two hours; buffs – fifteen to twenty minute soak and one hour mellow; browns one day soak and one day mellow. Mellowing means to allow the water on the surface of the rod to penetrate uniformly right through to the pith.***

***These key points are culled from a paper delivered by David Jones and Cyril Johnson at a Willows in Wales Conference held at Ynys Hywel Countryside Centre and Blackwood Miners Institute, Blackwood, Gwent on Noveber 22nd 1992.***

***J. Johnson & Son Basketware Specialists – a family business spanning five generations – is at Station Road, Bangor on Dee (Bangor is-y-coed), Near Wrexham LL13 0AB Tel: 01978 780 417***

# The Basket Makers Association

*Formation Aims and Benefits.*
*Sally Goymer – inspirational membership secretary*

The Association was formed in 1975 to promote the knowledge of basketry, chair seating and allied crafts. Also its design study and technique. The general concern for the environment, and the interest in using traditional renewable materials to create beautiful and practical objects for daily use, has seen its membership grow to a thousand worldwide. Basketry in its widest sense is part of the association's remit. The interests of the professional and amateur alike is catered for, be it as basket maker, collector, historian or simply keeper of a traditional craft.

A stimulating highly professional Newsletter reflecting the association's broad interests is published quarterly : featured titles have included 'Chair Seating in Hull, 'Hazel and Chestnut Basketry of the Pyrenees', 'Packing Tape Baskets' and 'Wicker Giants'.

As an organization it has an Annual meeting every October for the purpose of electing officials and a committee, and a Summer meeting in June, which is held at different UK venues. There are twelve thriving regional groups in the UK, and a database is maintained of those who accept commissions or teach.

A wide variety of courses are run at all levels throughout Britain, in addition to the City & Guilds and Chair Seating Diploma. All courses are open to members and non members, the emphasis being on the transmission of traditional skills to enable the student to develop a high degree of competence, individual style and technique. There are several bursaries awarded each year for further study, formal courses, research or travel. Further benefits of membership include : access to training videos, literature and a slide library ; two annual courses in Spring and Summer, and a handbook with members contact details and interests.

**The Basketmakers Association Enquiries Contact is:**
Rae Gillot, Glenwayth, Hervines Road, Amersham. Bucks. HP6 5HS

**The Membership Secretary is:**
Sally Goymer, 37 Mendip Road, Cheltenham. Glos. GL52 5EB
* ***The Complete Book of Basketry Techniques*** by Sue Gabriel and Sally

*Sally Goymer of the Basket Association shows examples of her work.*

Goymer. Published by David and Charles. SBN 071 539424 X

It is worth noting that Sally Goymer, the Basket Maker Association's membership secretary, who co-wrote this book with Sue Gabriel is an internationally recognized authority on the subject. It was a collaboration between Sue Gabriel the writer, craft enthusiast and educationalist and Sally Goymer which brought the book about. Sally, ever a hands on practical sort of person, had followed her basket making passion which had started via a City and Guilds course (with Barbara Maynard) and a persistent knocking on doors crusade, with a year of intensive training at the International School of Basket Making in France. She was already a competent basket maker at that stage, but ever the perfectionist, Sally Goymer needed to know more. And it was while idly fingering a French book on basketry that she stumbled on the course which was, as it turned out, to be held in a remote country village. She knew of the French standing in basketry ; whereas here in Britain it was a skill in serious decline, in France mainly as a result of the cooperative tradition, there was a school of excellence. Was going there an impossible dream? She was a married woman of thirty eight with two teenage daughters. And what of the cost? It was more than her husband and family could be reasonably expected to bear. And how would they manage if mum was not on the scene to fetch and carry and sustain the household? They were supportive but financing the escapade was a problem. But now she had the bit between her teeth. So it was more Knocking on doors in a quest for a bursary or grant – but alas no doors opened. Then at a Basketmakers Association annual general meeting she made an impassioned appeal outlining her case. And on the following Tuesday, a call from a member to tell Sally that her one year course in France would be financed and her traveling expences covered. Sally protested 'I couldn't possibly repay that' but the caller insisted 'this isn't a loan' and pressed on her to accept. 'Cinderella you shall go to the ball!' She admits now that the generosity overwhelmed her. The donor insisted on anonymity, and true to his word the funds were found, sourced by various members – many donating their course fees.

Sally now regards the course in France as a momentous event in her life. There in the depth of rural France living a rather Spartan life ; her living quarters a ten foot by ten room with a bed and a wash basin, with just one single window which was way above her head. But for that first week gripped by sheer exhilaration Sally was in her seventh heaven. Absorbing the course which entailed forty hours a week of intense tutoring and painstaking practical activity. Here she began to understand basketry as an exact science and enjoying every minute. This was no haphazard doddle – this was serious basketry at its most precise. Each move was practiced over and over again ; getting it right once was not enough nor even ten times – it had to be a hundred, even a thousand times. Lesser mortals might have given up. But not Sally Goymer. She admits now that the isolation and loneliness, particularly at week-ends when her fellow students went home because they were comparatively local, was devastating. Meals which were taken at the school common room during the week didn't occur then and she was left to using a primus in her room. And she sorely missed her family. How were they managing? Cynics among her circle shook their heads – 'here was another marriage going on the rocks' they murmured. But they needn't have worried a bit on that score. 'Here we are all together twenty years later' she says. In fact they learnt many lessons about dependence and interdependence. 'My girls learnt that being a wife and mother does not mean that you're chained to the kitchen sink'. And she proved there was life after childrearing. The book was the result of all that she learnt in France, a collaboration with a fellow Association member.

'After this it was obvious that I should share what I had learnt because I was the only person from this country who'd been to the International School of Basket Making for a year' she says. At the outset Sue asked her, if she had a choice, what sort of book would she really want? Sally's views on that were very clear. 'I wouldn't want a pattern book – how to make a log basket or how to make a shopping basket' she said. 'What I would want is all the different ways to make a base or border or a weave or whatever. Then I could pick out what bits I needed to make, the basket that I'd decided to make.' It was a formula which worked. To Sally Goymer's surprise the publishers printed 7000 copies ; she was aghast because membership of the Basket Makers Association all tolled was no more than a thousand. In the event they were all sold out in eighteen months – necessitating a further print run which was again sold out! It then came out in paperback.

So Sally Goymer is right at the hub of the Basket Makers Association with its world wide membership, ready willing and able to give guidance and help. Hers is a clearing house on the latest in festivals and courses. Places to get the best Somerset willows or basketry equipment are right at her fingertips. But it's her basketry that takes precedence workaday in her state of the art workshop and enjoying every moment.

## Further books recommended for basket making studies

*The Complete Book of Baskets and Basketry* by Dorothy Wright (Published by David and Charles, Newton Abbott.). ISBN 0 71538547X

*An Introduction to Basket Making* by Lynne Edwards (Published by Silverdale Books). ISBN 1 856 057 42 9

*Baskets and Basket Making* by Alastair Heseltine. (Published in the Shire Books Series by Shire Publications). ISBN 0 85263 611 3

*'Handmade Baskets From Natures Colourful Materials* by Susie Vaughan (Published by Search Press).

*Willow Work* by Mary Butcher (Published by Mary Butcher, 6 Downs Road, Canterbury, Kent.) ISBN 0 95255410 0

*Willows of the British Isles* by Teresa Breadell (Shire Natural History Series) ISBN 0 852637659